CATCHING WILD

Arizona

A. A. Lawrence

Copyright © 2008 by A. A. Lawrence.

ISBN: Hardcover   978-1-4363-6667-0
           Softcover   978-1-4363-6666-3

All rights reserved. No part of this book may be reproduced or transmitted in any form or by any means, electronic or mechanical, including photocopying, recording, or by any information storage and retrieval system, without permission in writing from the copyright owner.

This book was printed in the United States of America.

To order additional copies of this book, contact:
Xlibris Corporation
1-888-795-4274
www.Xlibris.com
Orders@Xlibris.com
30371

CONTENTS

For a Few Feathers 9
Signals 13
To Stand Among Them 17
Winter 19
The Knight 25
Heebie-jeebies 29
The Law 41
Dig a Hole 43
How to Bag a Jeep 45
Chicks or No Chicks 49
A Lure 51
October 53
Roper 57
Spurred 59
Sunchasers 67
Trophy Tree 77
The Gorge 83
Pike 97
More Bucks 101
Ludicrous 113
Collared Peccary 117
Little Shiner 123
Tangled Up 127
Goose Shoots 133
Right of Passage 137

Author's Note

I was born in Arizona over fifty years ago and have lived in the northern wild parts since. I have traveled to and traversed so many mountains, prairies, parks and valleys, canyons, and ridges and I crossed the rivers, swam in and waded through the mud cattle tanks, creeks, and waterholes that sprinkle them in quest of some sight or animal or bird that I can not recall all of the names of them, although I have vivid life-changing remembrances of what happened while doing so.

I have been asked repeatedly to tell these stories so I decided to write them down. These stories are true—the events really happened and were witnessed by others of whom I have fondly tried to protect by changing their names or by referring to them in different terms. This work is lovingly dedicated to those who were brave and courageous enough to walk with me throughout this passage of time.

For a Few Feathers

I feel cold lying on the snow huddled around an old fence post. I am waiting for sunrise and for feathered jet-like birds to soar overhead. I remember why I am here but am wondering why I had to get up so early to wait in the dark and lie in the snow for so long. I realize that my anticipation is high and I want to blast the sky with my Winchester semi automatic 12-gauge shotgun. I know that the excitement will warm me up.

Hopefully, I will get one or two today. I mentally coach myself. Hold the gun steady. Lead the bird. Keep both eyes open and shoot before they fly out of range.

I can hear them coming now; wings whistling. Do not look! If I look, they will flare and disappear into the low hanging fog. By the sound of their wings I know it is time. I shoot well and the bird is plummeting out of the sky with folded wings, spinning like that gun-shot fighter plane I saw on the History Channel the other night.

My partner is pleased with me. He says, "That was a great shot. Wait to get it! They are coming around again." We hunker down and wait for the exact moment to stand to take our next shots.

The next two hours seem to vanish into the past almost like they had not occurred. I finally realize that I am shivering and so cold that my fingers have stiffened around the barrel of my gun. That is enough for me. I have to get out of there and fast.

I need to cross the pond again, gather my ducks, and get to the truck. The thought that I was hypothermic crossed my mind. But I tell myself, "You got in here, you'll get out!"

My boot sticks in the muck. My foot is drawn up next to my chest and the boot is still stuck. Down into the ice-cold depth I fall. Amazement would not describe my shock when the breath in me left as I peered through the watery surface to see blurry ducks flying over. My gun looks particularly strange sticking up out of the water. Drenched would describe how I am but that word does not come close to how I feel.

I plow out of the water with all my might, straight up, trying to catch a breath. I hear him scream, "Get down!" I wonder what in the world his priorities are. I decide that he is dumber than the stupid ducks flying by. Does he really think I am going to dunk myself out of sight again so he can get another shot?

Trudging to make my way to shore, all I can concentrate on is that I am tired. I keep falling into the drink. The humongous wader-boots are sagging lower, the straps around my neck and on my shoulders are as taught as they can be, cutting into my tired muscles. I contemplate an attempt to reach my trustworthy Swiss Army pocketknife so I can chop off the feet or at least poke his waders all over so that they can deflate into tight spandex-like skin. The plan exhausts me just thinking about it.

My gun is dry. It crosses my mind to hurt him. Obviously, he is not focused on what I believe to be important—rescue. Would a thought to assist cross his pea-brain? Does he not know any sympathy? I loose my balance again. This time the fall does not feel so shocking. In fact, it is warmer in the water than out. I crawl to the shoreline and roll over to lie down. In that position, I recall him saying how much fun this experience would be that only confirms to me his lack of understanding the sensitivity and delicacy of a woman.

I bet I stripped myself in less than five seconds; leaving on only my most intimates. I decide immediately that I really do not look great in black-brown lace. The sliminess reminds me of Crisco shortening and it is all over me.

I do not believe it when he screams for me to hide from another flock of ducks heading our way. This time I scream back, "It does not matter if I hide anymore; there is nothing white or shiny showing that you have to worry about." I added that I am in perfect camouflage. If he bothered to look, he could see that!

I emptied the waders, tied my pants together by the legs so that they could be wrapped around my neck, tucked my gun under my arm and started dragging the waders behind as I quest for the truck, heat, rest, and relief of some sort. It seems like a long way to the top of that ridge. I rest a minute on the damp ground as I climb under the barbed wire fence. My bare feet hurt from walking on the sharp rocks. I do not feel too chilled but I know that is because the duck-mud is drying over my skin and I feel numb. I have a sense that I probably will survive.

That sense became unreal two seconds later when I saw the truck. There is something very weird about the truck. Its white color is blotted with something. I cannot find any reality in what I see. My breath leaves me again but not from drowning. My partner was angry with me and I do not believe he will come to rescue. He would think I was making up some sort of trauma to punish his evil treatment towards me. I scream for help anyway.

Amusement and laughter and hysteria overwhelm me. I am in another predicament that I have no control over. I perceive the happening extremely rare and unique. There are truly thousands, maybe a million tarantulas on that truck, under the truck and around the truck.

My banshee-type shrill got his attention but he does not believe a herd of tarantulas is after me or that the big hairy spiders are all over his white pickup. I see a million of them and they are going to get me.

Sitting down on a rock, shocked, nearly naked, frozen, and frightened I knew I would have to wait until the Angel of Lord knocked him in the head. I think that same angel will have to drag him up the hill too.

I scream again at the top of my voice aware that I am still dripping black goop, and shivering, "Come here! Now! You must see this! And you should save me!" Guilt got him or the Angle of the Lord smacked him. I am not sure, but I do not think it was my screams that motivated him. Most likely, the ducks stopped flying, settling on the water to feed and rest so that he could not shoot any more.

The sight of him strolling up the hill gave me some relief but not much. As he drew nearer I could tell that his eyes were squinted. His stroll turned into a slow gate, then a trot as he began to make out the unbelievable. When he reached me, it was his turn to feel terrible, guilty, and somewhat ashamed for his delay. His apology was lame.

He took off his jacket to wrap his arm for protection before he preformed his manly chore. This I watched closely and I vindictively laughed when the first swoosh across the side of the truck door causes hairy spiders to scatter everywhere including his shirt, pant legs and boots. His reaction was to jig, and shake all over. Visualize a dog shaking after a swim except spiders were flying off his body instead of water drops. He said something that sounded like major cursing but I could not be sure. I was still standing barefoot on the rock a long ways away and the wind had picked up. I watched precariously as spiders hit the ground and scampered elsewhere. I wondered, will I ever feel comfortable, warm, or relaxed again?

Thirty or so minutes pass as he fights tarantulas for our space. It is a huge herd. The ground appears to be moving. Some are trying to climb and jump back on the truck. Others are herding up together and appear to be organizing a march. Some leap from rock to rock. I am amazed at the different colors from light or sandy brown to pitchy black. The hairy spikes shine in the sunlight. I suppose, because of the excitement and being thrown onto the cold ground, partially snow covered, several are humping up and down on all eight legs or is that a greeting or sign of agitation and aggression?

He pleads with me and promises that it is finally safe to enter the truck and warm up. Reluctantly, I approach the truck then I get inside. As I do so, I demand that he get my outerwear from the rocks were I left them draped. I strip the other two little items from my black body. I notice I have bikini stripes distinguished between mud and skin. He gets inside the truck. He turns on the ignition, sets the heater on high and flips the fan switch to high.

Whap! Something hits me on my cheek, then another between my legs, then another on my bare belly. The old '55 Chevy is throwing-up stuff and spitting at me. The fan is spitting out furry, big, crawly, creepy spiders! Plop! Whap! Crawly, big hairy things are scampering all over my naked body!

I dive out of the truck as quickly as I can get the door open. I hit the ground landing on hands and knees. I scream so loudly that it scares every living creature for miles around but especially my partner. I stand and run like the wind across the prairie, naked, hands and arms floundering over my head, like that will scare the demon-possessed spiders off of me.

It seemed like a very long time before he tackles me throwing me to the ground on top of one of those sticker bushes. I am probably still in shock and I fight him. He tries to tell me that the spiders have flown off in my dash for deliverance. He explains that it took him a while to catch up to me because he had been overtaken with laughter that caused him to fall and roll on the ground. I finally do believe him because I am exhausted and do not have another sprint of energy in me. I recall laughing and crying at the same time.

We make our way back to the pickup. He tests the heater fan to be sure leftover flying tarantulas would not appear. He checks the floor and under and behind the seat. I even saw him run his hand through the back seat crack and he looked into the holes where heat comes out. It is all right because I can see the herd as a dark cloud moving across the ground. They are far enough away for me to know this duck hunt is really over.

We look over our dead ducks: three mallard drakes, a teal, and two redheads. My cloths are draped over the defrost vents on the dash of the truck. That is when I decide I am not going for ducks and feathers again—never.

Signals

It was one of those early fall kind of days, before any hunting season opens. We decided to just get into the truck and go knowingly taking risks that we will not need something—such as the tire jack that I remember is sitting on the workbench.

We were about to head home after foresting for a couple of hours and he said, "Let's take a short walk on the edge of that canyon to see what we can see." I commented that a short hike through a rich and old forest is the perfect thing to do.

Red-barked ponderosa pine is an indication of old, and that plenty of moisture has ensured a fast, tall, mature growth. If you smell the bark of a red-barked ponderosa it smells like delicious French vanilla. Its fragrance leaves if you take the bark from the tree. It does not do anything for your coffee either.

There were a lot of acorns that year. Even the bush-corns had a crop. Birds and animals including deer, elk, turkey, and bear eat acorns. Of course, I think their choice to eat acorns is like choosing a bitter green apple instead of a red-ripe-juicy cherry. Wild grasses look and taste much more delightful to me than acorns.

My mind was cluttered with such thoughts and my concentration was on the evening warmth, the last wild flowers blooming at my feet, that sunset would be particularly spectacular tonight and what I was going to fix for dinner.

He had wondered a little distance in front of me to peak over the edge. He had just commented that sometimes, an animal will go barely over and under the edge of a canyon where they feel safer to sleep, eat or just watch everything around them.

He then signaled me with an out-turned palm of his hand, a previously agreed to signal that means to wait where you are and do not move. You see, you just do not talk out there. You will scare all the animals away. You need signals. Even so, the signals change every time and in every situation because it depends on how talented the signaler is at playing charades. Everyone knows a signal is only a good one when the receiver interprets it correctly.

I am waiting patiently and contently leaning on and sniffing a big red ponderosa while anticipating the sunset watching him and waiting for the come-on signal. He is holding his binoculars to his chest and leaning way over to see all that might be just under the cliff edge. His head is sort of bobbing in and out like a turtle's head going in and out of its shell. He is bent over at the waist nearly forming a right angle with his body. I thought how comical he appears. I was watching him from his left side. A very large overgrown acorn bush—oak shrub—was directly to his right side. He did this animated posturing over and over.

Then I noticed movement and saw the tall antlers of a deer! It was a big mature buck, an Arizona mule deer, five-points on each side. The antlers are wide and because the top of the ears are just under the curve of the rack, I knew it was a real big one. He is directly standing on the other side of the big oak-shrub bush; right next to my partner. Their bodies cannot be more than 30 inches apart which I estimate to be less than the deer's antler spread.

The deer stepped forward just a little, and is looking exactly in the direction that my partner is—over the edge and straight down into the canyon.

Well, look at that! Deer can bob their heads in out like a turtle just like my partner can.

My partner popped his neck out again then turned his face to the left. At the same time, the deer pops his head out in front of the bush and looks to the right. Partner popped his head back as if into its shell and the deer's head pops back behind the bush again at the same time. With eyebrows high, both man and animal continue in the same manner turning their heads from side to side until all of a sudden they are head to head, eyes to eyes, nose to nose, breath to breath—only inches from the other face. That is when they both jumped straight up like a child's jack-in-the-box popping out with a racket of noise.

Obviously, neither of their brains had connected to what their eyes were seeing. They were shocked into solid ridged statues for a very long and funny moment. In the next second, the sight of being so close or in the heat of each others bad breath, my partner and the deer both jump forward which caused me to jump because I feared they would fall over the cliff. Each was barely able to back-step to avoid the fall-off. Rocks and dirt tumbled down. I recall the click-click-click-swoosh noise as forest debris fell.

Regaining balance another look at each other was the natural reaction. Their eyes met, bodies froze and jaws dropped open. Reality must have struck their brains but their physical reactions were clumsy and hilarious as each turned away from the other and ran away in opposite directions as fast as they could move their legs.

After a few leaps over huge rocks, dodging trees and scraping through bushes, my partner was overtaken by his experience and fell to the ground in plumb frolicking laughter. His gaze was fixed on the deer that had stopped to look over his back. The deer gave his head a big shake like a dog shakes when getting out of water, as he looked back at the man rolling on the ground. That is when that deer-buck grinned. Then he snorted and trotted away into the sunset.

"Why did not you signal me when you first saw that deer munching on the bush?" he asked.

"Tell me, what signal would that be?" I asked.

The truth is if he had bothered to look my way he surly would have realized I was signaling, sending messages by back-scooting up and down against the tree, laughing silently so hard that my face had to be bright red, pointing and dancing a little jig. Signaling through nonverbal body reactions caused from extreme excitement, but I truly doubt that he would have understood the signals even if he had looked.

To Stand Among Them

We were walking unreasonably fast. I felt very cold. The weather reporter stated that with the wind chill factor, it would be well below zero most of the day and a good five hours had passed since sun-up.

I look at him and cannot help thinking how amazingly fortunate we are to find ourselves here, now. His eyebrows have ice cycles on them and his mustache is stiff and snow covered. I wonder how that can even happen because breathing causes my lips to feel quite warm. I laugh out loud. I must be a sight to look at as well, because my own cheeks are not moving as easily as they usually do; they are probably frozen. I feel conscious of how feeling cold enables one to feel every inch of the body. It makes me happy to feel cold and to be witness to the strange things that the forest reveals.

By early dawn we had placed ourselves atop a ridge so that at first light we could observe any movement at its base. Nothing stirred. It was too cold for even the birds to fly from their perches. I was glad to move on until we were standing just inside a thick tree-line bordering a forest park. I thought about how gorgeous it was. Snow glistening in the sun, the mystery of the outdoors seeming to scream, "Look at me. Remember this for I am beautiful!" So I did. About that time a slight movement caught my attention and life changed.

Oh my! I see a twitch of an ear, a big ear!

My first thought was to signal my partner. It is my belief that every set of partners have prearranged quiet signals but which one do I use for this? I tried to whistle but nothing more than a gust of air came out between my lips. I tried again but it did not work. I cannot clap. I cannot talk, I cannot even move or everything will be ruined. I have a gun. Why do not I just shoot it? They are too close. My scope is set too high and I cannot move to adjust it.

I want to scream at my partner to ask if he is deaf, dumb, and blind. I wanted to ask, what does it take for you to be in-tune to your surroundings and why can't you sense that I am excited or even sense their presence? Even though he was not more than five feet from me I could not reach him. I even tried ESP. I figured five seconds of thinking real hard should cover five feet. Instead he was concentrating on the view through his binoculars.

Several minutes had passed since I first realized that we had mysteriously walked into and remained in the middle of a snow covered, slumbering herd of elk, about 40 of them. How long could this last? The sight alone made me know that it is worth being born for. I was alive and overwhelmingly pleased to be. A bull elk with a majestic rack of six points on each side lay six feet from my left side. There was another one, closer yet. I could have sat on her. The bull stirred, raised his mighty head and turned to look at me. A stream of foggy breath leaked from his nostrils. He licked his nose. A reflex that I knew would sharpen his smell. His ears flickered then he yawned. The other elk, a herd of both cow and bull were waking. They flexed their bodies so that the snow that had accumulated on their skin while they slept glided off to make little piles of snow around their sides. I did not know elk slept so soundly.

I slowly, but barely moved while I looked for the sentry or look-out. Every herd has one just like a flock of geese does. The sentry was on the other side of the herd and was lazily rising to his knees. He would be fully alert in a matter of seconds and he was more majestic than the one still laying to my left. As he stood to full height he shook like a wet dog does coming out of a pond. Then he signaled the rest of his herd with a loud drippy snort.

I just could not contain my excitement any longer. My partner was still missing it all. I had to let him in on this secret now! I moved quickly and grabbed his arm and twirled him around to face the sight. This shocked him and he even looked angrily at me. One second later we were both standing in amazement and a type of reverence came over us because of such close proximity to such magnificent, majestic animals so beautifully formed.

The elk allowed us to stand among them another few minutes as if we were amusing them. Then the herd gracefully turned in obedience to their leader and slipped out of the heavily treed grove and over the horizon.

I still wonder how an elk, even a small elk can move through a forest of thick jack-pine ponderosas not to mention their Houdini disappearing notoriety. I wonder where do they go, why we cannot see them when they are there, how were we able to walk in the midst of them and I wonder why they let us stay there for so long?

Winter

Winter was too long this year. We had moved to the country last spring and we were not ready for the break of a nine-year drought and the house was not sufficiently weather-proof to sustain us comfortably. After completing expensive repairs on the old furnace and burning eight cords of firewood, the newsman is reporting that it is suppose to warm up to a real heat-wave of 60 degree days soon. That will be nice but I doubt that it will feel warmer with the 60 mile-an-hour winds that he says will accompany the higher temperatures.

During the last days of February it snowed three feet in 4 hours. We lost all power, water and electricity for 47 hours. Our power supply is electric so the toilet does not flush; there is no shower, no cooking stove, no electric lighting and especially disturbing to us, no television to help make the hours pass a little more quickly. Our cell phones would not even pick-up a signal.

We live in a ranch area where only three full-time residents live; our neighbors where in a worse situation because they had no provisions or camping equipment. We had just returned from a week-long elk hunting trip that enabled us some comfort because we still had supplies, fresh propane canisters, and five gallons of water that had not frozen into a huge ice cube.

It was most important that we keep the fireplace burning twenty-four hours a day because our plumbing had already frozen to slush. We burned as hot as we could and kept all the cupboards open trying to circulate the heat. I was wrapped in blankets even so. You could see your breath when you exhaled. It was cold even right next to the fireplace. In bed with all the covers on, I did not feel chilled.

I was most thankful for the water and the little propane camp stove and the old stainless steal coffee pot that we retrieved from the barn. The sound of the pot perking is still a strong comforting memory from my childhood. Do you remember Mrs. Olson's kitchen and the Foldger's coffee advertising jingle? That is what it was like.

The old propane lanterns, we had two after we had given the other two to our neighbors, were flickering a very deep golden light all over the ceiling and walls. That reminded me of fluttering fairies; the Tinkerbelle kind of fairies. That was pleasing to me.

There are a couple of skylights in our want-to-be modern, revamped, dressed-up old ranch house. It was almost comforting in a strange way to watch the snow flakes hit the glass, melt and dribble down the rounded bubble tops until one started leaking a steady little stream on to the carpet and countertop. That called for a couple of cook pans to catch the water. Pretty soon it sounded like a little melody was playing: plop-plop, perk-perk, patter-patter, and swish. The high winds in the pine tree tops provided the swish and a scrape sound. I noticed the snore of our sleeping dog and crackles of burning wood added something to the menagerie of tones and feelings I was experiencing. A little bit of cabin fever starts to settle in after twelve hours but it has not been all bad.

By the second morning, we had managed to clear the front gate but realizing there would not be any vehicles going or coming we did not uncover the front porch. The chickens were alive because we made a little ten foot path in the snow for them to strut back and forth on. Otherwise, they got stuck in little holes because when they tried to walk on top of the deep snow they would fall straight down surrounding themselves in vertical tunnels. Chickens get very up-set when they can only see the sky or in this case white flakes coming from above falling on them. It is very scary to them and they flop around in a tight circle in the hole, screeching and yelling until they exhaust themselves into shock. We only let that happen one time; poor little bird.

I remembered that I should be concerned because I had not seen my partner for many hours. That reminded me of what happened just after we had moved in.

There is a corral on the property and inside the corral are three stalls built into solid rooms on the outer part of the barn-garage out-building. The stall doors are spilt halfway up so that the top part swings out while the bottom part stays locked and closed. They are the kind that Mr. Ed the talking horse, used to stand behind and stick his head out of when he talked. We have never had horses or stalls. We thought it was odd that there are no latches on the inside of a stall but I did not think too much about it until my partner disappeared.

I was in the house unpacking. My partner was outside looking for something. The newly installed telephone rang and I was surprised because I did not even know the telephone number or that it had been turned on.

When I answered the phone a man said, "Lucy, I am in trouble. I am stuck inside of a stall because the wind came and slammed the door shut. It is real dark. I cannot get out. Come save me!"

I almost hung up, wondering, "Who is Lucy?" Then I remembered our new stall and that sometimes my partner calls himself Ricky. With that thought, I knew that another calamity—something funny had occurred.

If my partner did not have his cell phone with him he would have stayed locked inside that stall for hours. I may have remembered him if he did not show up at dinnertime but I am not sure about that.

I just heard of a man, a rancher, who was digging a deep narrow hole and he fell inside of it head first. He was stuck like a cork or corn cob up-side-down for seven hours and nearly died from a head-rush or suffocation. His wife came home early and pulled him out of that death trap hole. With that in mind, I threw on my down coat and boots and went to check on my partner and that saved him that day. About then I realized we had a lot to learn about this new environment and country living.

Before Ricky got locked into the stall he had found 250 feet of orange extension cords. Who in the world keeps 250 feet of extension cord? That is twelve, 20 foot cords and one must have been 30 feet long. What does he need those for? I wondered.

Our neighbor had managed to get out using 4-wheel drive, a winch, and chains and had traveled 200 miles on snow packed roads to find and buy a generator. By then, my partner had managed to clear most of the snow away from the driveway in front of the barn-garage and was then going to help our neighbor start the generator and if it powered his house, then we could plug in all of our cords to power our house if the generator had the power to do so.

The neighbor received a report that said power would not be restored to the area for another twelve to twenty-four hours. It was still snowing heavily and the temperature would drop severely that night. The temperature was nudging up to the 30 degree mark at 2:00 p.m. so, that meant it would be well below zero that night.

Temperatures and weather like we were experiencing is not really unusual for the area although, not to be prepared for it can be very dangerous. A community being caught unexpectedly is even more dangerous and threatening to the people who live in it. We were in the latter situation and we were beginning to realize that other people were actually in life-threatening situations.

Our neighbor reported that a couple of young kids were stranded in a cabin two miles from the main road. If they attempted to walk out to the main road it would be another 3 miles from anything or any possible help. They had no water, heat, wood to burn, no food and no one had been able to reach them. Hunters were stranded in the wilderness, their vehicles buried in snow and mud, rescue vehicles buried, and others for miles around us were desperate for help to reach them. Then to make matters much worse, temperatures would drop and the snow would continue. I felt terrible.

As we were talking and trying to think of something to do to help we heard a deep rumbling sound over the ridge just west of us. A huge bulldozer peaked over the far ridge road. We wondered where in the world it was coming from. It came to a stop in front of our place and a big fat cowboy got out saying, "We brought this brand new rig up to the ranch last week and I decided it must be good for somethin' but I do not know how ta' run the thing yet." We could not help laughing.

Our neighbor, the one who got the generator, being a Harley Davidson rider, a lineman for the county, and unbeknown to us, a heavy equipment construction worker as well, stepped right up to the plate and said that he sure knows how to run the thing and he could clear the ranch if he could drive it all night to do some rescuing.

The cowboy rightfully agreed and was thankful because that is just what he had in mind to do in the first place. So that is what happened. Our biker-neighbor drove the bulldozer and cleared the big ranch's roads including the area where feed was kept for the horses, rescued the kids in the cabin and a couple of others, plowed our over-long driveway, his driveway and the main road in to all of our places.

Meanwhile, the men who were around got the generator running and both homes warmed up. They also made sure that more wood was placed in the wood box and stoked the fire. I cooked a good old fashioned camp dinner on the camp stove and eventually we all sat down together. The plop-plop, perk-perk, patter-patter, swish sounds returned, the dogs slept in front of the crackling fire and we watched the flicker of the lantern light dance on the ceiling and walls.

We thanked our Lord for finally feeling warm and for the tenacity and strength he gave us that day. We asked that he renew it for the next one too. Most meaningful, we were thankful for having each other. The winter will pass, the snow will melt eventually but how this time changed us in simple ways is everlasting.

It is amazing to me how day to day life can get so burdensome. I want to remember that if I look hard enough, there are true marvels that people

Heebie-jeebies

It was late summer. He and I had no schedule, except lunchtime had to happen for him so we always included that along with the play, talk, laughing and doing whatever made us happiest that day.

After some deliberation about what would be fun to do we decided to load the 4-wheeler quad into the back of the pick-up truck and go south until I thought of a place to ride it. All the way, he asked if he could drive the machine. I usually did not allow him to drive it because he drives too fast and it is against the law. He is only seven years old.

We did not have helmets or pads or other protective gear because we did not need them. The quad was intended for hunting expeditions and for retrieving animals after a hunt not for zooming down dirt roads going as fast as one can go. Even so, we both knew the quad could reach high speed and it was quite a laugh to make it do so.

Finally I turned off the highway and headed to a place on the Verde River called Brown Springs. Brown Springs is at the end of the old Salt Mine Road just outside of Camp Verde. When the paved road ends a rough dirt road continues for 18-20 miles. It follows the river most of the way and coils down and up steep canyons. There is not usually traffic so it is also a good place to ride and we can skip off the road for a canyon exploration or to go down to the riverbank to sit or get wet and cool off for a while.

This day was going pretty much like that. We had gone to the river, traversed canyon sides, spotted and followed whitetail deer, shot a B-B gun at a jackrabbit, rocked, and bumped along for hours. I did not realize the time of day, as I usually do not when I am with him on some kid-like adventure. I guess that is because I can see things and feel things the way he does. We had no problems or worries. We took time to notice the gorgeous desert flowers, bugs, birds and the lizard on the rock.

Late afternoon came too soon and we headed back towards the spring's road. About a half mile off of the main road there was a little shallow creek bed that we had crossed earlier, farther down the canyon and closer to the river. This minor obstacle is not a problem for a quad. As I approached the little dry bank to ease the quad across he yelled, "Stop right now! You are giving me the heebie-jeebies!"

"What in the world is wrong with you?" I asked.

There was no argument. I just stopped and he got off. He can walk across the ditch if he wants to, I thought.

Down the side of the bank, over a rock and skip-pity-do-daw I went. Someplace along that little jaunt I was thrown off the quad and down the creek. I laid more than ten feet away from the quad when I dizzily looked at it and saw that the quad had become possessed. It was clawing itself up the other side only hindered by a jumping, thrashing giant bush, screaming and shaking for its very life. I must have passed out after that.

My next thoughts included: What in the world was that? I do not feel so hot. Quit poking me in the eye! Leave me alone! Do not even touch me. I might be dying!

He was poking me in the eye and as he lifted my eyelid he asked, "Are you inside there?"

"Of course I am in here. Shaken up a bit, but I am not lucky enough to have died and gone to heaven," I replied.

My reply scared the boy, he whimpered just a little. I felt sorry. Although, I was actually feeling irrational at the moment because I had no clue what had just happened to me. I hurt. My back hurt, my head hurt, I ached all over. And it did not help that he was holding my head up when I woke up and when I spoke he let go from shock and my head hit a big rock for the second time. I screamed and he jumped back, just not knowing what to do. I am not sure things could get any worse.

Gathering my strength and wits I managed to get up. I felt dizzy and the back of my head felt gushy but I thought I would be okay and I knew I had to act like I was, just for the kid's sake, not for any other reason. The quad was still bucking the bush and at full-throttle. I explained to him that it was possessed and that he needed to stay back and away from it while I tried to tame it and cast out the demons. He said "Okay," and he did so.

I grabbed the possessed thing, jumped on it and turned off the key. I actually took out the key from the ignition but it did not turn off. I clutched, squeezed, and braked. I tried shifting gears, pushing it, blocking it and kicking it. It just kept going. After several more minutes passed in the same state of possession, and my tenacity had nothing to do with it, the quad puttered, coughed and died all by its self. Even though it overwhelmed itself to death, I felt like I have after a great hunt and the kill when I would be jumping up and down and doing a jig. I had the same sense of victory, one that is not comparable to most events in life. It is special.

At that point, I realized that I had lost my glasses, my prescription sunglasses and the sun was hot and shining in my eyes. Still I tried to muscle the quad upon the bank so that I could try to work on it and get it started again. Working on it means that I would jiggle some things that stick out. I have no clue what really makes a quad act like it does. I realized that was no use before I even attempted it. I already knew that the little guy and I had a long night and a very long walk back to the truck.

We took a few more minutes looking for the glasses but we could not find them. I decided the throw I had felt was probably strong enough to have tossed them down to the river a mile away.

He was messing around the quad and I asked him what he was doing. He said that he needed his gun, his B-B gun, if we were going to spend the night out there he would shoot dinner.

I told him we needed to leave it with the quad because I could not carry it and he could not either, not for that far.

He cried crocodile tears and said, "His Pops would never leave his gun in the woods and he would not either!"

I asked him to think about that. I tried to explain that it would take us all night to walk back to the truck and that there were lots of canyons to climb up and down. And that we should get started on our way, but first could he get the Gatorade and the little bottle of water because we would be taking that along with us. I was improvising a carrying pouch thinking that I wished that I had that cell phone and the jacket and the package of jerky that I had left in the truck but I did not mention those things.

All this time our Dayzee was beside us. She is a sweet, all terrain, strong-hunting Labrador retriever. We needed the water for her and she would protect us from snakes and during the night, I explained.

He got the stuff. He left his gun. When he came back to me he said, "Take my hand, I will help you up the hill to the main road. You will be feeling better after that."

After we had walked about a mile he asked, "What are you getting for dinner? You have to because you made me leave my B-B gun."

"Oh, we will dig up some worms, find some bugs and eat the inside of a cactus and I might find a few plant tuber roots that taste a little like potatoes," I answered.

He just said, "Okay." After a little while he added that he was not all that hungry yet, as if eating worms was some everyday thing we did when we were out and about. I hoped that he miraculously just would not get hungry. Finding normal food in the wilderness of any kind can be quite a challenge. I wished that I would have let him bring his B-B gun.

As we walked and walked and walked on, my mind was drifting and stuck on the time when he was only 16 months old. I had taken him to the woods to cut some small trees to skin and make a log bed out of. As I was cutting the little guy wandered a little too far and I told him he must come back, now! He yelled back that I should come to him because he was "walking with the deer." He announced that just as he reached the top of the ridge and walked out of my sight.

When I got to where I could see him again I was amazed. He truly was walking with deer. He was only 14 or 15 inches tall and there he really was walking right beside, close enough to pet the doe and two little still-spotted fawns.

Walking the road, my thoughts returned to the problems at hand. I was worried about that little people get dehydrated faster than adults do because they do not sweat. I made him take a drink and realized that he was flushed and too hot so we had to stop and rest under a big cedar tree beside the spring's road for a while. It was about 4:00 p.m., the hottest part of a day in summer.

We talked about how to tell time based on the position of the sun. I explained using my arms for examples. It is like the hours on a clock just that the hour points are above you in a line starting at sunrise being at your feet and as time passes, the hours go over you, noon being straight up. The difference is a clock goes right to left or around the hours on a clock face, noon being straight up. Our shadow is a good gage of time also. I figured that is was about four o'clock. We had walked about four miles. We had a long ways to go. It would be dark before we knew it.

My butt hurt badly. It was pretty swollen and that made it hard to walk. I was thankful for the break but I also knew that I would become stiff if I sat there much longer; we should move on now.

I knew that Brown Springs ranch was closer from where we got stuck than the truck. I was wondering if I should have gone there. But it is the other way down the road, about three miles. There is a little cabin there and food and water. The Ranch family runs cattle in this country. We know the family well but I also knew that they had the cattle round-up a couple of weeks earlier and it would be very unlikely that anyone would be there. I reasoned that taking that way would be a greater risk because that would mean that we were walking farther away from transportation or the likelihood of meeting another human being.

We walked on but slower than before. We were getting tired and needed to rest more often. I wanted to get out of the canyon, upon a ridge before making a fire because canyons are colder during the night than on top. We also would have a greater chance of seeing lights from a vehicle.

I knew it would be a few hours but eventually, someone would notice that we did not make it home and would start a search. I had told them, sort of where we were going. I was hoping someone would try a little ESP and figure it out even though ESP had never worked before, I always suggested it. I hope that if you are close enough to someone, they could think real hard and sense things, places, and feelings of another. I think it is true between my young side-kick and I.

I was also hoping they would remember to get us a big old fat double cheeseburger or chips or make a peanut butter sandwich before they left civilization. A beer and about 20 Aspirin would be good too.

I did not talk about my hopes with him but I figured he was thinking the same things. I was pretty sure that he was resigned to the thoughts of bugs or those things I said were sort of like potatoes. He is so faithful to whatever I tell him. I sort of felt guilty about that for a minute but then I knew I would not let him down and I suppose he knew that too.

We topped the ridge and I announced, "We were camping out now!"

"Let's get some firewood and I'll look for some grubs for dinner while we do that." Dayzee even helped him gather some firewood by picking up pieces in her mouth and carrying them to the place I was getting ready.

"I am not really, really hungry yet!" he announced. "We would not have to eat bugs and other stuff if you had let me bring my gun. I could have shot us a rabbit and we could have stuck it on a stick and cooked it in the fire."

He was right and I told him so. What was I thinking?

He did not know that a B-B probably would not kill a rabbit unless he hit it right in the eye at close range. I sure wish he could try. He was mad, reminding me that we would already be home for dinner if I had not been so stupid to break the quad. He added that his mom was probably going to be mad at me and that for sure Pops was going to be mad for breaking his Quad. Then he said, "Papa is going to have to ground you, but not me, because I did not do anything bad."

He also asked, "Why did not you listen to me when I got the heebie-jeebies? It means to stop and go another way," he explained.

I responded by telling him that I did not get the heebie-jeebies this time, and that he never said he had those before either. How was I supposed to know what it meant? I thought, poor baby. That is when I suddenly could see humor in the whole incident and our circumstance.

I started laughing right out loud, grabbed him, hugged him, tickled him, and we just had a great time laughing and rolling around on the stickery ground. I realized that moment, these are indeed the days of our lives and that this one-day-alone was probably the best one ever.

We were just getting settled into the fact that we were stuck, alone, and still happy, and most importantly together when I spotted a little flash, sun reflection on the far ridge. I pointed the spot out to him and asked him to keep his keen eyes on that place.

"It is probably just a piece of broken glass or a shiny rock catching the sun but you just never know what it might be," I said.

Dayzee barked. Then we heard crunching sounds. Then it nearly scared us into shock as this biker turned the sharp curve just to our left and went zooming past in front of us.

It took two seconds but I stood up and yelled, "Hey! Hey you, Stop! Please!"

My screaming scared him so much that he jerked and nearly rode his bike right off into the canyon but he did not. He was standing there holding his chest with one hand. We just stared at him. I was a little embarrassed to ask him for help after scaring him so badly.

Little Guy, standing right beside and looking up at me said, "See? You just gave that guy the heebie-jeebies too."

The biker was a lot older than I. He looked so weathered. He had longish grey whiskers, steal blue-grey eyes, he was skinny yet very athletic looking and he was dressed from head to toe in black spandex with a blue stripe on the arms and down the legs. His helmet matched perfectly.

"What in the world are you, and a kid, and a dog doing out here, sitting on the side of the road?" he asked once he caught his breath.

Before I could reply the little guy starts yelling, "My Nan is in trouble! Not me! My Nan is because she was stupid and broke my Pop's quad, and she made me leave my gun, and then she says that I have to eat bugs, and that we have to stay here. She is in big-big trouble!"

He or I could not contain our laughter after that proclamation; I could only jester that what he said was in fact the absolute truth.

I asked his name. "Doug," he said.

He explained that he rides his bike the full eighteen miles in and out everyday. He has never had such a fright as we just gave him. He asked if that was our white, super-cab Chevy truck, parked another 9 miles up the road?

"Yes, that is our truck. Is it really another nine miles? We are kind of in trouble but someone will be looking for us soon. We will rest up a little and when the moon comes out we will just keep walking that way," I rationalized.

I continued with introductions, "This is my grandson. He is only 7 years old. Say hello to Mr. Doug and tell him thanks for stopping."

Before he could do as I said, I interrupted, "By the way, do you happen to be carrying a cell phone?"

He said he did.

I was so relieved.

He handed me his cell phone. It had a good clear signal. I immediately called home. Pops was upset when I told him we needed help. He was busy and frankly, he did not seem to know if he could leave his work right away. He was still at least two hours away even if he could leave. This seemed to be a great inconvenience to him. I was obviously bothering him or a bother to him.

I asked him to call the child's mother and I hung up the phone. I figured she would not be so nice and she would make him do something or she would do it herself. I could not help wondering where his priorities are. I could not believe that he would leave us to ourselves to deal with the problem. His rejection shifted my focus. No relief after all. My bruises and hurts seemed a little deeper and painful.

The little guy and "Mr. Duck," the name he immediately dubbed the gentleman with because his name sounded similar to duck, were having a nice conversation when I approached them. Mr. Duck had given him a cracker or something and had made sure that he drank a lot of ice cold water. He even gave Dayzee some water. They were talking about "dee-hy-der-a-shion."

Mr. Duck glanced at me but continued to explain that it is best if we always carry water and drink little mouthfuls very often. That is why his water bottle is on his back and an attached straw was close to his mouth so he could slurp a little, often.

The boy replied by explaining that he and his Nan always take water but not with straws and that sometimes his Nan forgets to take lots of food and he was going to be sure that never happens again. He was telling Mr. Duck about his B-B gun and that he could shoot pigeons right out of the sky when he hunted with Nan and Pop. He said he almost could not miss when he shot at the same time as his Pop or Nan. "When that happens," he says and he nods his head a little, proud and amazed, "The birds just fall right down. Then Dayzee gets 'em and brings 'em to me."

Band-tail Pigeon, Kelsey Spring

Mr. Duck wanted to know the rest of the story and what exactly had happened to us. He had overheard part of my phone conversation and did not seem too happy with the outcome either. Then he said that he would ride his bike back to our truck, put his bike in the back and drive our truck to us. I handed him the keys. He peddled away leaving us sitting on the side of the road, under the tree just as he had found us.

A long time went by. We settled into our spots with Dayzee laying her head on his leg. I told him stories of the old days, about times when I was a kid. Things like the first time I shot a rabbit and how it used to be okay for us to have play guns. We played cowboys and Indians in the big granite rocks in our back yard in Prescott. We wore our guns all the time, even when we ate dinner or played marbles. My double holster pistols had fake-ivory grips. Those were the best.

Thinking about my kid-days reminded me of a trick my grandfather taught me. You cut a little twig from a live cedar tree, skin the bark off, and then you suck on it. It keeps you from feeling thirsty. I did that for him and myself. Not that we were thirsty right then, but that is what you do. I let him do it by himself the second time. He liked the feel of my pocketknife in his hand and he whittled our little sticks meticulously.

It had been so long since Mr. Duck had left that the thought of him stealing my truck and driving to Mexico had crossed my mind more than once. I was relieved when I could hear gravel and rocks popping under tires. It was Mr. Duck, the little guy was sure. I was expecting to drive Mr. Duck home to wherever that may be. Instead, he insisted on going back to where the quad died in the creek. I let Mr. Duck drive. We had walked the Brown Springs Road for 4.5 miles that afternoon. Mr. Duck said it was 8.5 miles to the truck from where he turned back to get it.

As we bumped down the road the way we had just walked from, the little guy said that he was sure glad that he did not have to eat bugs for dinner but that he would have if I had found some. He thanked Mr. Duck for coming back because his "Nan said that she thought he had stole the truck and drove to Mexico."

We parked the truck at an old cow-watering tank close to the ditch that I had left the quad in. When we got to the quad it was just how we left it, half-way up the steep part of the wash, back wheels half buried from it trying to grab dirt in a huff-puff jump to the top before it died.

Mr. Duck muscled the machine like any man would and somehow managed to jam the gear into neutral. The released quad rolled down the creek bank and the tire would have squashed our little guy if he had not leaped into the dirt away from it. I was so tired by then that I just flopped to the ground and I half cried and half laughed from relief and I really did not care if I got the quad-thing home or not.

Everything stopped and it was quiet for about two seconds. I thought I heard a put-put-put sound. I declared that it sounded like the quad's twin. We all listened very intensely for a few more moments and agreed that the sound was getting closer to us. I ran up to the top of the hill in spite of my aches and pains. When I arrived there, I waved my arms and hands and called for the rider to stop. When he did it was obvious from the put-put sound that there was another one approaching.

As I walked toward the rider I recognized him as one of the Ranch boys. My, I was surprised and instantly knew I had made the wrong decision to walk toward the truck instead of the ranch house. Oh well, how could I have known that the boys were riding the range on their quads looking for rogue cattle?

They explained that there are always a few bulls that are missed during the round up and they were there to try to find them. The others in the cattle drive where on horseback riding high-country.

Knowing me and the tales told, the rancher asked, "What are you doing out here and what did you do this time?"

"Oh, just riding. Then we took a four-and-a-half-mile walk for fun, after the quad threw me and killed itself doing it. It is broken and stuck down in ditch and we cannot get it out."

By then our little guy and Mr. Duck had joined us and we all started laughing again. Shortly after that someone said that we should go and check out the damage done to the quad. They looked at it, tossed it, roped it, pulled it, and talked to it just like they do to their own horses. With much effort and the determination of cowboys riding bulls, they eventually managed to get the quad started again and to stick the gear in reverse. It only went into reverse there was no questioning it. That is when I witnessed something I knew I would never forget.

The quad was not only stuck in reverse it was also stuck full-throttle. So when one of the Ranch boys jumped on it, it burst up the other side of the creek bed backwards and jumped up over the ridge at high speed and it bounced the cowboy like he was riding a wild bronco. The dude looked like he was holding on for dear life. His expression was one of fear and shock not that he was really feeling either.

He got closer to the truck where someone had already placed the ramp on the tailgate and I knew he was going to try to zoom it backwards right up the ramp and into the truck. He missed the first attempt and just zoomed around and around the truck three more times. The dust was so thick that we could not see the rider. I wondered if he was doing that in hopes that the thing would run out of gas or just decide to kennel-up like a dog does after a long day of retrieving birds.

Two more cowboys joined us and they were laughing so hard they could not speak. It was Mr. Ranch and another of his sons. They seemed be sizing up all the commotion as they looked around, at the same time doing the cordial things by greeting me and Little Guy and their good friend now known as Mr. Duck, and working in the question of how he ever got to be involved in this.

They had witnessed the scene from upon a ridge and rode down to see what all the commotion was about. I told them that quad was possessed and they believed me as they watched the quad rider spin around the truck in billows of dust once more.

That is when the other boys decided they had better give their brother a little help with the capture of the beast and they ran to grab the quad as it whipped around again. They caught it alright but they could not hold it for long by its tail so they both jumped up on the sides and each took control of the break mechanisms one on the handles and one was jumping up and down on the foot break until the quad sort of stopped, at least it slowed down.

After another rodeo circle, they somehow managed to get it lined up with the ramp to the truck bed. Two others were already in the truck bed poised to do something, and I wondered what that would be. I guessed it was just in case they needed to catch it. The men let the quad go up the ramp into the bed while holding it back with all their might by hand and ropes. We all are still sensing trouble, but we are amused and amazed and giggling.

Sure enough, the quad's front left tire, which was on the tailgate down-side fell off the ramp. That is a real scary thing to experience, dangling there with the danger of a possessed 500-pound machine falling on top of you. It was all the boys could do to stay gripped to the brakes as the rest of us wrestled to get the quad back on track and avoid the spinning tire.

"Now that is what I call having the heebie-jeebies," I said to the little guy standing beside me. He shook his head in agreement. He did not seem to be able to talk at the same time as watching the circus events happening in front of us.

Mr. Ranch had gotten his rope off his horse to do something when the quad finally jumped up into the flat area in the truck and the rider jerked the key out of the ignition. This time with the key missing, it stopped.

It took six guys and a lot of muscle to tame that quad that day and to get it resting safely in its corral-truck-bed. They were pretty brave because as they did it, the quad had jumped the sides and they managed to throw it back in. It hit the back window and another guy just shoved it down with his boot. Mr. Ranch needed the rope after all because the quad did not settle down until it had been hog-tied to the sides and caught in the tire chucks.

Finally, we were standing on the ground beside the truck. The boys shook off the dirt form their pants looking at each other with grins from ear to ear. They did not say a word, instead in unison they looked at me and Little Guy and Dayzee who was sitting beside me wagging her tail. I interpreted the looks as saying, "Girl, look at what you did this time. They should not let you out, ever." In truth, I knew I had accidentally given all of them a time of their lives with the heebie-jeebies or not.

At this time, Pops drove up. Guess he had a change of heart. He missed everything and he did not have any food but he had a beer, several that he passed out to everyone. Even Little Guy had a swig. Perhaps that was his first taste of beer and I figured he deserved it.

Little Guy and I and Dayzee were riding again the next Saturday after the mechanic had fixed the broken driveshaft, the tires, and filled it up with gas again. That day, neither of us got the heebie-jeebies and we made it home in time for dinner.

Little Guy, Zachariah Vosberg Day Lawrence

The Law

Our neighbor ran into a doe-deer on the road late one night last January. He called the county sheriff's office to ask what to do and they put him on hold and never answered again. Then he called my husband who told him, "Just load it and bring it to our house." Late that night we cleaned the deer, then packaged it up the next morning.

When the butchering chore was done, we loaded the big black gut-bag into my truck. I took it to the shop dumpster in town the next morning.

A couple of days later, I pull into my son's water company to visit with him a moment and right behind me pulled in a police officer. My son and the officer started chatting; I decided they must know each other.

The officer turned to me and seriously asked me, "Where is the body?" And he pointed to my truck, and the dry blood that had run out of the truck bed and through the tailgate.

I answered, "It was just a road-kill. I dumped the mess early this morning." And I added, "If you want to know more about it, you will have to talk to my neighbor. My neighbor called the Law when it happened. You can talk to my husband about the details, but he has been gone for a couple of days and I am not sure when he will be home, exactly."

I must have sounded like a blabbering idiot just talking and explaining that the Law is never around when you need them. It would have been stupid to leave it there. There did not seem to be anything else to do. The incident was not my fault. I had nothing really to do with it at all.

The officer just stared at me and shook his head back and forth. It took a moment but that is when I realized that he must be thinking that my neighbor and I had ran over and killed my husband—the road-kill.

I stood there silent with big eye wonderment thinking about what he must be thinking about. The officer pulled out his pocket knife and twirled it around in his hand for a second. It was his move; I bit my tongue so I would not say more.

That was when my son finally told the guy that I was his mother. The cop decided not to take scratches of blood for the DNA test, as he planned to do.

Then the officer started telling me about a body he found in a suitcase and the way he found it was a pull-over after noticing what looked to be blood dripping out the back of the vehicle. He explained that he pulled me over for "probable cause."

My son casually got a water hose and began to wash the blood out of and off my truck, ridding the "probable cause" and evidence. Even so, the officer insisted that I telephone my husband. He sounded relieved when my husband answered the phone. The officer stated that he was glad to hear him sounding well. He did not ask any other questions. I suppose he just did not know where to start or what to ask.

The officer left us standing there kind of miffed as he drove off in answer to a radio call.

I wondered what in the world would happen next, out here in this peculiar little country community. Who would have thought, that a run to the dumpster could turn into a "probable cause" murder investigation and that I was the number one suspect?

Dig a Hole

Another day and other hunters tell the outcome of their storytelling with the addition of some seasoned wild advice for a listening rookie. They told him that if he wanted to get an antelope, that he needed to go find a prairie where the antelope run, dig a big hole in the middle of it, get in the hole with his gun and stay there no matter what, until he hears the sounds of hoofs running, then to just pop-up when the sounds were close, and shoot the biggest one.

It took three days, digging rocks, some rain, bailing water and mud out of the hole, freezing mornings and evenings, and lots of Vienna sausages and hot coffee, but the rookie did just as the old guys said to, and it happened just like they said it would. The rookie got the biggest antelope that season at 15 yards from his hole with bow and arrow.

Being some years later, this antelope is still bigger and better than any the two storytellers, advice-givers have bagged. That is because neither of them would ever do such a thing, even if it may work: "Dig a hole in the middle of a prairie and stay in it until they hear the sound of hoofs running across the prairie."

These rookie stories prove that wisdom and experience are not needed before becoming a hunter—they are gained while trying to be one. With a little luck in the draw, guts for going, an attitude that risks are for taking, and some tenacity, living is not normal any longer. It can not be after the hunt because it changes perspective forever—life really does become just a little backwards and up-side-down and sometimes hilarious more often.

How to Bag a Jeep

He was only seventeen years old. He never had been hunting and he had never shot a gun. He had heard-tell of the excitement and adventure others found hunting, and he specifically recalled some stories that the old guy told about hunting in Arizona a long time ago. Even though he felt he lacked wisdom and experience and someone to go along he decided he would put in for the bull elk hunt and if he got drawn for a hunting permit he would figure out how to do it and get a gun. A few months later, he got the permit of his dreams in the mail.

The night before opening day he tossed and turned, feeling excited and thinking the next day of his life could be the best one yet. He was up two hours before dawn, pacing, checking out his barrowed gun, checking his pockets, going through his pack, the regular things a hunter does before he begins his hunt. Finally it was time and he got into his little CJ-5 Jeep and quietly left his normal life behind.

Once in the hunt area, it was not long before he spotted a herd of elk, standing and milling around about 75 yards away. He pulled off the road a ways, turned off the jeep and noticed the moment the engine stopped the elk jumped and ran away. He decided to track them but never caught up to the herd again that day.

The second day, he knew exactly where to go—the same place and with any luck he might see them again. There was a nice six-by-six mature bull in the herd and he dreamt all night about him. But he decided that he would be real happy to just get a shot at the smaller bull, a nine-point if you count both sides of the rack although, in Arizona we describe the size of antlered animals by counting each side, calling it a five-by-four, which is not trophy size.

Again he found the herd. In the same place and the bull was just standing there. The moment he turned the engine off, they ran away and disappeared into the timber again. On the third morning exactly the same thing happened and by now he knew better than to chase them. He needed a new plan.

The fourth day of the hunt, he returned to the same place and sure enough, the herd had returned. He figured they must like the grasses and he also knew that a watering tank was not too far from where they were feeding so it most likely was not just his good luck. He felt like he was learning something.

This time he decided to leave the Jeep running in low gear, as he scooted out the driver's door. The Jeep kept going, just jerking along at a slow speed bumping up then down into the old ruts in the road. Pretty soon his Jeep was out-of-sight because it bumped and jostled and turned a little bend in the road. Oh well, he thought, I will find her later.

The elk were in range and the biggest one was standing there, behind the herd, no cows in the way, hot steam shooting out of his nostrils when it exhaled, lips slightly curled getting ready to bugle, it stomped his right hoof and the frosty-speckles of dew on a piece of grass flew up and sparkled in the morning sun.

As he watched and readied himself he sensed more, smelled more, heard more, felt more than ever before. Steady, aim, safety off, keep both eyes open, squeeze—do not pull, he reminded himself. Bang! One shot! Reload and do it quick! He was pretty amazed that he could even pull the trigger because he was shaking so much that it was hard to take aim and steady the gun's weight. He even felt a little faint because he had forgot to breathe for a long time.

The elk dropped in his tracks. Great shot, he could not believe it. The big thing just laid there, did not move. The rest of the herd did not even run away, at least not until he started moving toward his trophy. What an elk! The bull was a lot bigger than he thought and as he stood over the massive body it occurred to him that he really did not know exactly what to do next.

He knew he had to dress-out the animal and never seeing it done before, he just logically started at the end of the belly. He did the best he could and finally, the animal was cooling out as good as could be expected. Within a few more minutes, he decided that it would be easier to hang it from the heavy branch of a big Ponderosa pine tree to skin it out or quarter it or something. It was too big and heavy as it lay. He could not even roll it over, there was no way he could lift it without using leverage.

He tossed a rope over a heavy branch, tied the other end of the rope behind the antlers and heaved. He heaved and heaved and heaved some more but could not lift the animal more than a foot off the ground while trying to keep a tight grip on the rope and slack out by wrapping the rope once around his waist then his hand. After a few minutes more of heaving and contemplating he remembered the winch on his Jeep.

"Oh man, my Jeep, where is my Jeep? It has been more than an hour since I shot my elk and then some time passed before I even did that. Holy Moly!" he said out loud.

His trophy was such a great one and even though he had not seen another person in four days, he had the inclination to kind of hide it after he tagged the antlers. So he did that, before he started tracking the Jeep. He had heard stories told about somebody else stealing trophies as the hunter retrieves his vehicle or finds help. That is a heart-wrenching thought.

As he walked along down the rutty road, he sort of laughed at himself but on the other hand, he figured he had been pretty clever about tricking the elk herd by leaving the Jeep running and going on all by itself.

It was a couple of hours later and six miles farther before he heard the Jeep's engine still putting and whining. The whining was because the Jeep jumped the ruts and caught itself in a barbed wire fence. He retrieved it and drove it back to where his trophy waited.

He slung the winch hook over the thick branch, wrapped the hook end around the base of the antlers and caught the hook around the winch cable. Then he returned to the Jeep to reverse the winch into rewind. As the cable tighten the gear dropped into a lower gear mode but the weight of the animal was too great. He needed to lift as the winch pulled. So he did that. The elk rose into the air and right when all the weight of the animal was off the ground, it reversed and eased back onto the ground.

All this time he was in such concentration and physical stress he really was not watching the Jeep as it was working but when the elk dropped down then laid on the ground again, he could turn around. Low and behold! The Jeep was dangling totally off the ground and lifting higher, hanging by the winch cable, swinging back and forth.

What in the world was he suppose to do now? He sure had not heard any story about a predicament like this.

He could not reach the ignition keys to turn the Jeep off or do anything about the winch still running; the mechanisms to do so where too high. He hoped the winch would burn out, break or just stop; it was smoking. He reasoned all that he could do is to wait until he had some undreamt inspired idea.

The sun was setting and while he thought he gathered some firewood. Should he get another idea, he would need a little extra light and staying warmer during the night would be nice. Nobody knew what he was doing or where he was exactly. Somebody might drive along eventually if not tonight, tomorrow he hoped. Even if that did not happen, he would figure it out.

As it came to pass somebody did drive along that road that night. Two old rusty cowboys had taken out after their meal to check that their fence gates were closed. This is something cowboys have to do because hunters in their pursuits, too often do not close the gates behind them. Livestock, mostly cattle escape their fenced free-ranging lands and can become lost assets to cattlemen.

The cowboys turned the bend in the road where the Jeep had gone the other way then disappeared earlier. These old boys were dumbfounded by the sight flickering in firelight before them. What they saw in that light was a young kid starring into the fire with his head kind of down and draped behind him, a Jeep hanging in a tree. They could even see a cable hooked to the elk a little to the left of the kid because the antlers were so big and sort of glistened and caught the fire light in just the right way to be visible. The truck driver could not take his eyes off the sight, and started laughing so hard that he almost ran into the tree in front of him.

"Whatcha' think is goin' on here, Joe? Sort-a looks like somethin's turned out a bit backwards."

"Well, it dern-neer looks like a young whipper-snapper has done bagged a Jeep. Or, is it that elk who done the baggin'?"

"Well, I think y'er right. For the laughin' we're bound to get out of it, let's see what his story is."

They casually strolled up to the kid, like cowboys always do. They did not say a word, just handed him a Coors beer, and looked at him then the Jeep until he started explaining. And, he did explain and explained and explained. The cowboys laughed and laughed and joked a little too as he did so. Then the hunter asks them what they think he should do when the sun comes up, to alleviate some of the problems he has encountered.

Of course the cowboys had all kinds of suggestions like leaving the Jeep hanging to season-out, cutting the tree down, eating some of the elk until it got light enough to give way to the Jeep. All of which the rookie hunter thought were excellent ideas and he just wondered why he had not thought of them.

The cowboys eventually chained the backend of the Jeep to the front bumper of their four wheel drive, three-quarter-ton ranch truck, pulled it to the ground, hanging the elk, then skinned the elk in a proper way, cut out the poison glands to dispose of them rightly, and sent the hunter on his way to make more stories yet to behold and be told.

Rookies should be aware that wild game have poison glands according to the old-timers and if you ask one to help you clean your game, the back straps and tender loins will mysteriously disappear because these delicate glands need to be disposed of rightly.

Chicks or No Chicks

It is just another day in my life.

I gathered eggs. The hens are laying eight to twelve eggs a day and they lay them at 10:00 a.m. When a hen lays an egg, she squawks and cackles and struts around fluttering her wings and wagging her tail.

Last night the power went out and my incubating chicken eggs froze. You need to keep temperature at 99.5 degrees at all times. When the power went off I had no idea that the incubator would not reset. This morning the incubator thermometer reads 65 degrees.

It takes twenty-one days for a chicken to hatch. When the temperature drops the baby chicks may not be able to peck through the shell and suffocate or they may be damaged perhaps missing claws or worse.

I called my friend, a veteran chick-hatcher and he said give it another seven days and while you wait collect new eggs to start the process again. That does not sound promising.

He also said to candle all of the eggs. I am waiting for it to get dark because you cannot see the chicks inside the eggs during daylight. He also said that I could just crack one or two open and then I could see if something was growing inside. I am not going to do that.

Our neighbor ordered some birds from a place called Murphy's. The twenty-four turkeys arrived last Wednesday. I guess we paid about $8 per bird. We only ordered twenty but they sent twenty-four because some always die, we have lost three so far.

Our neighbor built a super chicken coop condo that includes three levels for the birds to rest on in his yard with an old skylight as a window. He will feed and watch all of the chicks until they get a good bunch of their feathers. Once they get their feathers they become very hardy and strong birds, before then they are quite delicate.

Henrietta, our hen turkey has laid eight eggs so far this spring, we ate four before she started sitting on them. There are not any eggs left because a crow came and ate them when Henrietta got up to eat a little of her scratch. When that happened, Henrietta went to her nest and one-by-one picked up the four broken eggs and took them outside the stable to the corner and kicked dirt on them. Then she went back to the nest and tried to lay another egg.

We think it was weird that she just cleaned it all up and resumed her nesting because chickens do not do that. I have decided that I like turkeys more than chickens.

Henrietta is sitting on the nest now but I do not know if she has any eggs. I learned that all turkeys lay a clutch of eight to twelve eggs in spring. On one day the turkey hen decides to sit on them and she does so for twenty-eight days. The eggs all hatch at the same time. Last spring her eggs disappeared one at a time; it was a bull snake that got them last year, not a crow.

On Tuesday evening, we decided to go sit a wild turkey roost that we had found the week before, until dark to see if a gobbler would come. We sat there perfectly still for two hours. I sat on a hidden sharp rock and was not comfortable. I was thinking about where to move to when a huge bird flew into a pine tree only a few yards away. The bird purred—a give-away that it was a hen. We were so hopeful that more birds would come into the roost but they did not.

The wild hen jumped around in the tree tops, kind of jittery while making very soft chirp sounds. We could see her very well and her behavior was interesting. After a little while she flew away. It was an exciting eight minutes and I suppose that eight minutes made it worth all.

A Lure

Lake Powell, Arizona is the finest fishing place in the world, I think. We were trolling from a twenty-four-foot little cabin cruiser about midday.

"Once I fished up a big ol' rubber boot. I am going to tie a great big ol' bomber plug, a sky blue one with a yellow belly, on the end of my line because I am tired of having to toss and toss this light-weight and I want to sit here and do nothing for a little while," I said to the captain.

"I'm snagged up again. You'll have to back up or make a wide turn so that I can retrieve my lure. It is one of Granddaddy's and I do not want to loose it," I declared only minutes into my first bomber cast.

"Try pulling it; reel-in. It may come loose because we are in very deep water and I do not think there is anything to snag on, except maybe a sunken ship or a body," he ordered. I did not like the second descriptive possibility but I tugged hard and reeled.

I worked hard for at least five minutes while captain was making a big swing. Then, way out there, a dolphin jumped and when it did my line slacked and jerked. Now I know there are no dolphins in Lake Powell but the thought would not leave my mind's image.

"What is that?" I screamed.

Captain yelled, "That's not a boot! You got a big one! Get away from the edge of the boat so it does not pull you in! Keep your pole tip up! Do not allow slack! Just reel!"

"Oh brother, this is sort of scary—and this thing is probably a heavy-heavy spinner dolphin!" I screamed back. "Whoa!"

My mind was tricking me with all kinds of illusions: like being swallowed up like Jonah in the whale's belly; like being pulled around the lake making a four-foot splash that flies up on each side of my body as I skim across the surface, leaving a huge wake in my path; to seeing the headline news on channel 10 describing an old lady catching the sea monster in Lake Powell who almost died when the monster swung her against the cliff wall, but she hung on and lived.

It took me thirty minutes to work that thing hooked on my granddaddy's lure close enough to the boat to be sure it was a huge-striped bass.

It took the two of us to lift it. When we got it aboard the fish was longer than the sea chest pushed up against the stern. That ice chest is about four-and-one-half feet in length. We pulled the ice chest out and laid it upon the top. The head and tail of the bass hung over the edge of the sea chest.

"Holy Moly!" I screamed, as I rubbed my sore biceps.

Then we did the little jig again, the captain and I hold hands jigging around that big ol' fish in a circle—just giggling and giggling like very young children.

What a fish!

Lake Powell, striped bass heaven

October

We went to the North Rim Grand Canyon in the Kaibab National Forest and hunted grouse for a week. We got eight birds and that is not too good but average compared to some other hunts during previous years.

Grouse are illusive little birds about the size of a prairie chicken, two pounds in weight. They flush like quail which scares me, hindering my naturally, ordinarily fast shooting ability. They fly very fast. The shooter must lead them by 1-1/2 to 2 bird lengths. They disappear in an instant, flying into very deep forest of juniper and fir. They are extremely camouflaged and there are not very many of them to begin with. With all of these hunter handicaps I feel very good about killing two of them myself. They are very delicious to eat. The eight birds we got could be priced out at $100 per bird when the expense of the hunt is considered. No wonder I consider grouse to be a great culinary delicacy and that is why I do not like to share them with others.

Two other hunters went along with us. We slept in a camp trailer; they slept in their truck, which made me the provider of all other things. I like tent camps better because the camp becomes more of a co-operative effort, a help and provide for each other condition.

One of the campers fixed Somemores, the graham cracker, Hershey chocolate, roasted Marshmallow camp cookie, and that was nice although, I experienced a major sugar rush so I did not have anymore Somemores after dinner because I am sure they give me bad dreams and make me jittery and they make my heart pump too fast for too long. Somemores just are not the thing for me to eat for breakfast or lunch either. I ate jerky while the others ate their Somemores after the first time.

Last week there were six men in the house for seven days; they were seriously archery hunting bull elk.

On day two of the hunt, one of the archers shot a five-point bull at 30 yards. Two hunters were hunting together that morning, one the archer and the other used an elk call to try to lure the elk into range. It was an amazing experience as the bull bugled all the way into range then the bull stood still and looked magnificent lending the opportunity for the excellent shot.

During the next two days, the successful archer and I butchered and wrapped the meat. Then he went home and the other hunters stayed although, they were not successful at finding or sticking an elk during the final three days.

This Friday, is opening duck. There are three different hunters coming from Tucson tomorrow. I will not go along because I do not like duck hunting anymore even though, it will be the first opening day duck hunt that I have missed in ten years. Something terrible always happens to me during duck hunting at Lake Mary or on the Mormon Lake mesa. If they decide to hunt ducks tank-jumping on Saturday, I will go along.

Tank-jumping is done by driving to a water tank or pond that may have ducks sitting on it. The hunters get out of the vehicle and sneak up the bank or through some other type of cover. If there are ducks on the pond, they will fly at the least sign of intrusion and that is when the hunters shoot at them. It is a fairly successful method of hunting ducks when there are ducks.

On October 20th, the cow elk hunt opens. I have never hunted cow elk even though I have killed four bull elk. The primary purpose of this hunt is to take a ten-year-old on his first-time hunt. He completed the eight-week hunter safety course only two weeks before opening day and for that reason I am most excited for the hunt to begin.

Once the elk hunt is finished, there will be more duck hunting and Thanksgiving is planned. We will eat Henrietta for Thanksgiving dinner.

We are raising turkey: Nickel, Dime, Tookey, Buzzard and Rio are our new little turkey. They are eight months old and are all wild breeds. Tucker and Little-T are older gobblers. Henrietta is the oldest of the turkey. I may add chicken to the feast because there are eight hatchling chickens that the black hens brood. These chicks add to the total of seventeen chickens. The chickens have names, Monday through Sunday but when I had more than seven, I started using months as names. I quit naming them once I arrived to January. We ate Black January just last week.

On the day before Thanksgiving, we waited until the National Anthem was played at high noon then hit poor Henrietta in the head with a baseball bat when she was not looking.

Henrietta weight 35 pounds, oven ready. She was 18 inches high, 16 inches wide and 21 inches long. The Whitehouse was planning to serve a 30 pound turkey that holiday.

The problem I had was that Henrietta would not fit in my oven, even though I had taken all the racks out of it and shoved her in with all my might. I truly contemplated quartering her and called a friend in town instead, who had a commercial sized oven. She cooked Henrietta all night and set her alarm every two hours purposefully to baste the bird with a Bourbon and molasses and mustard mixture.

Henrietta tasted absolutely wonderful, and since then, I have replaced my oven with one that will hold a 40 pound turkey, not that I will let one get that big again.

Home grown, free range chickens are tough eating but tasty. They have no fat—a bunch of feathers really. They taste like a wild bird, perhaps like grouse with a touch of banded tail pigeon.

We will have to cull the flock before heavy winter snow falls.

Recently, a stupid full-grown 1000+ lb cow poked our chain linked fence and somehow actually picked it up pushing the top rails out of the caps and off, bending the chain link badly, and then plowed through and pushed under the chain link to get into the yard.

That cow ate the whole bail of hay and then experienced awful diarrhea. The hay that it ate was rotten but it sure liked it. The bail had sat there a year as we used it for a backdrop while target practicing.

The neighbor tried pushing the cow out using the four-wheeler-quad, but that did not work so he found two neighbor boys, ages twelve and thirteen who he talked into helping him. He told them it would be easy to get the cow out into pasture. Of course, after the boys agreed, it was the neighbor's job to observe and yell commands about what to do and how to do it.

The boys were really scared of the cow but they were determined to drive it out. They raked their bodies over the six-foot fence twice and one locked himself in that stall with no inside latch, for safety once. The cow's calf stayed on the other side of the fence, making a very irritating belly-aching noise. It was trying to get inside too. The cow tried to get to her calf but not seriously, because she was focusing on the boys' actions while she continued to eat anything sticking up on the ground.

Finally, the boys chased and cornered the cow into the coral area where all the chickens and turkey live. That caused another ruckus. There were chickens and turkey flying around, flopping wings beating the sides of walls, fence and dirt and making loud clucks and squawks. Two of the turkey flew the fence and landed in trees. The dogs had already done the initial scaring of the cow and were now kenneled-up in another area but they were barking, wanting to escape and to join the chase.

One of the boys shot the cow with his slingshot and that really angered the cow evidenced by a stand-off and scraping dirt with hoof. They feared the cow would charge, but it did not because it was a cow, not a bull. The cow was just pretentiously standing-off, a threat but no action intended.

The boys eventually quartered the cow off and because all animals, birds and humans were tired, the cow slowly meandered out the back gate and wandered back to its calf.

We removed the rest of the hay as not to tempt the cow back.

One of the boys and I spent two hours that evening repairing the chain-linked fence. It still needs stretched and it is high at the bottom but we will use rocks to block it. The red fox we saw the other day very close to the house would have no problem getting in, let alone skunk, raccoon, coyote, bobcat, or lion.

While we worked on the fence, the oldest boy asked me what I would have done differently.

"I would have put the rest of that hay in that wagon over there and taken it to the cow. Then I would have slowly pulled it out the back gate while it munched the hay along the way."

The kid was most thoughtful for a minute and said that he sure wished he had thought of that. He added that the whole adventure was one of the greatest times he has had so far. Then he decided that he was glad he did not think of that because it might have changed the day's events and the adventures.

He grinned and giggled and put his hand around my shoulder as we just gazed out and beyond, not seeing anything, just replaying the scenario in our minds.

I like range cattle. Even so, they keep the elk away, contaminate the wild game water tank that is close by, and now I know they do damage and they are very stubborn. Before this happening I thought it would be a good idea to raise a calf or catch an elk that I would keep in the corral. I do not think so any longer, as I remember the cow that went under the fence and another story about the roper.

Roper

My friend and storyteller who is adamant about remaining nameless, had the idea that he was going to rope a deer, put it in a stall, feed it up on corn for a couple of weeks, then kill it and eat it. The first step was to get a deer. He figured that since they congregate at this cattle feeder and do not seem to have much fear of him that it should not be difficult to rope one.

He filled the cattle feeder then hid with his rope. After about 20 minutes a deer showed up. He stepped out from the end of the feeder, and threw a rope around the deer's neck. The deer just stood there and stared at him. He wrapped the rope around his waist and twisted the end so he would have a good hold. The deer still just stood and stared at him. He took a step towards the deer and the deer took a step away. He put a little tension on the rope and that is when he started gaining his deer education. He explains:

The first thing that I learned is that while a deer may just stand there looking at you funny while you rope it, they are spurred to action when you start pulling on that rope. That deer exploded!

The second thing I learned is that pound for pound, a deer is a lot stronger than a cow or a colt. The deer ran and bucked and twisted and pulled. There was no controlling it and certainly no getting close to it, as it jerked me off my feet and started dragging me across the ground.

Ten minutes later, it was tired and I managed to get up. It took me a few minutes to realize this, since I was mostly blinded by the blood flowing out of the big gash in my head. At that point I had lost my taste for corn fed venison. I just wanted to get that devil creature off the end of that rope. I figured if I just let it go with the rope hanging around its neck, it would likely die slow and painfully somewhere. At the time, there was no love at all between me and that deer. At that moment, I hated the thing and I would venture a guess that the feeling was mutual.

I could still think clearly enough to recognize that there was a small chance that I shared some tiny amount of responsibility for the situation and I did not want the deer to suffer. I managed to get the deer in between my truck and the feeder—a little trap I had set before hand. Kind of like a squeeze chute. I got it to back in there and started moving up so I could get my rope back.

Did you know that deer bite? They do! I never in a million years would have thought that a deer would bite somebody so I was very surprised when I reached up there to grab that rope and the deer grabbed hold of my wrist. Now, when a deer bites you, it is not like being bit by a horse where they just bite you and then let go. A deer bites you and shakes its head—almost like a pit bull. They bite hard and it hurts.

The proper thing to do when a deer bites you is probably to freeze and draw back slowly. I tried screaming and shaking instead. My method was ineffective. It seems like the deer was biting and shaking for several minutes, but it was likely only several seconds. I, being smarter than a deer tricked it. While I kept it busy tearing up my right arm, I reached up with my left hand and pulled the rope loose. That was when I got my final lesson for the day.

Deer will strike at you with their front feet. They rear right up on their back feet and strike right about head and shoulder level, and their hooves are surprisingly sharp. I learned a long time ago that when an animal like a horse strikes at you with their hooves and you can't get away easily, the best thing to do is try to make a loud noise and make an aggressive move towards the animal. This will usually cause them to back down so you can escape. This was not a horse. This was a deer, so obviously such trickery would not work. In the course of a millisecond I devised a different strategy. I screamed like a woman and tried to turn and run.

The reason I had always been told not to try to turn and run from a horse that paws at you is that there is a good chance that it will hit you in the back of the head. Deer may not be so different from horses after all, besides being twice as strong and three times as evil. The second I turned to run, it hit me right in the back of the head and knocked me down.

Now when a deer paws at you and knocks you down. It does not immediately leave. I suspect it does not recognize that the danger has passed. What they do instead is paw your back and jump up and down on you while you are laying there crying like a little girl and covering your head. I finally managed to crawl under the truck and the deer went away.

grows. A ten inch beard indicates an old mature gobbler, a trophy for a turkey hunter. A Jake's beard is funny looking because the hairs just pop out, one at a time and stick through the feathers and the growth stays only 1 or 2 inches long for a year or two so it is easy to deduce the beard grows about one-half to one inch a season or a year. This growth does not look like something natural. Even so, the turkey beard could be compared to antler growth on deer or elk and a long beard is definitely a show of dominance in the turkey kingdom.

Another distinguishing feature of a gobbler is that they grow spurs that are used for defense and show. They grow about an inch above the foot on the back of the leg. They are triangular in shape like a shark tooth. They are boney and stiff and quite sharp but not as sharp as the point of a knife blade or a shark tooth. Again, the older a gobbler gets the larger and longer the spurs grow. When they fight, they jump up and stick out and up their feet driving the spurs into the chest area of their component.

Everyone knows of the great fan tail of a gobbler and that a gobbler will strut and fan, twirl like a ballerina on one leg, and drag its wings during the mating season to attract hens and show dominance. These showy features, defense mechanisms and the large size of a gobbler turkey all contribute to the components needed to live in the wilderness and attract hens and gather a harem.

Fall turkey hunts are the most difficult because you just have to find them feeding or hope to find a roost or catch a flock watering or crossing the road. During a spring hunt, gobblers will come to you in response to a lost hen call or purring call that mimics a content hen. Turkey actually talk to each other by making a range of sounds all day although, it is difficult for a hunter to hear the regular turkey chat because the sounds are soft. A hen will purr after she lays her egg for the day or is browsing through the forest and she will make the lost hen call when she becomes separated from the flock. There is also a call that mimics a "hoochy-mamma" almost saying, "Come here big boy." That call can scare a gobbler away but sometimes it is just the thing to persuade him to come closer.

During the everyday mating ritual flocks split up and wander around. A hen may stay within her own nest area. She may be alone or with two or three other hens each day until her clutch of eggs is large enough to satisfy her. Meanwhile the gobbler is making his rounds. That is why a hunter is most likely to get a gobbler to come to a call around 10:00 a.m. and because around that time he is more likely to pursue other hens outside of his own harem while his hens are laying eggs. Logically, it is also the time of day when hens most often make the same calls the hunter is mimicking.

I decided that turkey are really stupid and at the same time became fascinated with their behavior and socialization during my first turkey hunt, a fall hunt in 1970. This story really starts on the fall morning of day three.

We had spent the two days prior trying to find some birds that would cooperate with us and we saw turkey everyday except did not get a shot because they were too far away or they just ran away too fast and disappeared. More accurately, the birds were really too fast for us to get out of the truck, load our guns and shoot. We had decided that the hunt was really turning into a fair-chase hunt and that the birds were winning.

During a late spring scouting trip we witnessed an amazing turkey ritual. From a mile away we heard what sounded like tribesmen beating on large kettledrums. It was a deep, resounding, rich toned sound. Almost like a gong. The sound repeated every three to five minutes. We could not identify or even guess what the sound was because we had never heard it before or have since then.

We slowly tried to approach the area where the sound was coming from, the side of a fairly steep ridge where a landslide had occurred most likely during the previous winter snows or summer rains. In other words, it was a clearing on the side of a steep hill scraped of trees and bushes. A perfect place to observe what was about to happen.

As we approached the far edge the drum sounded again and we saw two huge gobbler turkey ramming their air filled hollow breasts into each other. The impact caused the resounding kettledrum sound. When they jumped up to hit each other, their spurs were clearly in view and as breasts hit, spurs jabbed deep and feathers flew. On impact both birds flopped backward falling down on their backs, wings flopping wildly. The birds gobbled sickly, more like a gobble-moan than gobble-giggle as they dizzily stumbled back to their feet. Then each bird did a little twirl-around jig, wings down and dragging with fanned out tails and puffed up sides. The two want-to-be-champions backed up from each other, faced off and charged with all their might again. They whammed into each other with mighty force and started the ritual, stance, strut, tough-guy show all over again. During the gobbler fight of a life time, there were 38 hens that I could count circling the fight—a circle of gaggling, screeching, jumping, twirling, pecking, flopping hens.

The show continued for another thirty minutes. The gobblers were obviously well matched in grandeur and strength. Eventually, one bird finally turned around and wandered out of the circle while some hens protested his defeat. The winning bird gloated by showing the width and length of his wings. He puffed out all his breast feathers and stuck out his beard. He swayed his huge fanned tail back and forth sideways, dragged his wings and stuck his scarlet-red head up high and turned in circles on his tip toes showing off his great spurs.

"He truly deserves that victory dance," I said out loud.

We stayed there watching until all the noisily talking turkey walked over the top of the ridge out of sight following behind the strutting-walking-twirling gobbler.

I felt exhausted. To watch that was just exhausting. The amazement I felt, the wonder and the understanding that it was an absolute privilege to witness such a happening, felt overwhelming.

The morning of day three we found ourselves in the same area where we witnessed the great gobbler fight. We were driving along a steep ridge, too thick with fern and mesquite, a thorny-type of bush on one side, straight down canyon on the other side, just road enough for the truck. It would be impossible to get out and stand beside it. My side was the stickery, bushy, uphill side. My window was rolled down so that I could hear well, see more, smell better and because it was too hot inside with a coat on and too cold to take it off with the window up.

A little break in the thick wilderness terrain was just ahead and when we reached it I heard a loud swish, crash then thump! At the same time something big and mostly black hit the front metal part of my open window then ricocheted onto the hood of the truck. I almost had a heart-attack. Something clicked in my mind and I realized it was a stupid turkey flopping on the hood. I realized the bird had nearly come through my window and if it had, I would have had that heart-attack and one heck of a battle with a big bird on my lap, inside the cab of the truck. Thinking about that, was as real as if it actually happened.

The turkey on the hood was a gobbler. The driver hit the brakes which threw me into the windshield and the turkey off the hood to the ground right in front of us. We, the turkey hunters are dumbfounded and speechless for at least two minutes. Coming to our wits we notice turkey all around us. Some had hit trees trying to dodge the vehicle I suppose, and some were still soaring overhead, and we saw some landing in the 75 feet high Ponderosa pine trees on the down side of us at the bottom of the steep draw. As if we just realized we were hunting turkey and that is what those things are, we jumped out of the truck with our shotguns unloaded and slid down the embankment in quest of those crazy, albatross-type turkey birds.

At the bottom in a little cleared valley area between the two ridges we began to search the tops of the trees looking for big clumps sitting close to the tree trunk. Everything was quiet. Not even a squirrel chirped. That did not surprise me because I had experienced shock and had not spoken since then and could just imagine how the other animals and the turkey were feeling, if they feel anything.

We spotted an unusual looking clump and stood directly under it trying to determine if it was a turkey or a pine needle squirrel nest. Squirrels make nests like that. My partner threw a couple of rocks into the tree but the clump did not move. Due to a slight change in the sunlight and a shift in viewing position and good binoculars we were almost convinced it was a turkey, enough so to consider shooting at it—considering the angle is straight up, the clump is 65 feet high, the angle needed to take a shot is nearly impossible while keeping the target clear of limbs. We considered more and discussed what to do and decided that I either have to lie down on the ground on my back and shoot or he could support me with his body as I lean way back with the gun pointed up at 180 degrees, to shoot. I decided that the recoil of the shot gun might really hurt if I was lying down and chose to use him for back support.

I shot. The clump flopped and tumbled down hitting limbs as it fell through them. It was a turkey alright! And I recall it as if in slow motion because the recoil had knocked me to the ground and I lay there peering straight up into the tree, flat on top of my partner who was squashed, unable to breathe underneath me.

Whap!

"Ouch!" I screamed.

We did not move for a minute because we had to think about what had just happened. There we were, lying flat on the ground, my partner under me, me on top of him, and one big turkey laying on my stomach on top of both of us with its wings flopped over both my sides. My gun was still pointed straight up with the butt resting on the ground and there were little tiffs of smoke rising from the gun barrel. The turkey fell right on top of me, on my belly, and it spurred half-inch holes into my skin. I think I am bleeding a little. Serves me right, I thought.

We finally got all arranged and up off the ground. Laughing like hyenas, we grabbed each others hands and danced a jig around the turkey in circles like playing ring-around-the-rosy. My partner pulled out a tail feather, picked my hat off the ground where it lay ten feet away due to the gun blast, and stuck the feather into the side, then he placed it on my head. The hunt was over, but never to be forgotten.

I was nineteen years old and that was the first turkey I ever shot.

My turkey was a nice gobbler with a 9 ¾ inch beard, weighing 20 ½ pounds. I got my picture taken at Ruff's, the place where all locals have their pictures taken when they get a big one. The store boasts an impressive hunter's trophy bulletin board and holds picture albums of people and their trophies taken over many years which still tell the stories and hold the evidence of never forgotten hunting adventures.

"Now, that is what I call a hoot of a hunting tale!" I can hear the old guy in the store say right before he took the snap-shot picture.

"A hoot for sure!" I replied with a big grin on my face, feather in my cap and a hearty giggle in my heart.

Sunchasers

Our quest was to go for an innocent Jeep ride in the forest. We were going wherever the sun was shining during that monsoon season. The sunshine was fickle that day. We chased rainbows north, east and west for the first hour. Southward looked most promising.

While I was trading my truck for the Jeep, I did tell the guardian, "I am going where the sun is shining." In my mind, that was being informative and responsible and explanation enough reasoning that if I were told that, I would look at the sky at the estimated time of departure to see where the sunshine might be.

He did not ask any questions. I know that he does not like me to just take off into the wilderness, often alone but that did not stop me.

I reminded him that I am a veteran of nature. "I am very in tune with survival tactics involving wilderness adventures because most of my experiences in nature have involved calamities that have at times been somewhat life-threatening; learning most while trying to live through them and getting home safely. And, most of time I was with you."

This day I took a ride-along who seems fascinated with my wild-knowledge. She is joggling along and seems to be experiencing the same bliss I am. This is new to her. She has never been off the black-top pavement let alone in a Jeep with the top off. To that day she had never seen a deer run and jump close-up, in the forest. She did not have a clue which weed was edible and she had never driven over downed timber in a vehicle. The thought of sun-chasing had never crossed her mind as something to do. Her enthusiasm, the newness of it was beautiful, fresh and enlightening to witness.

We came to the end of a ridge over looking a deep canyon—the continental divide that separates the Ponderosa treed north mountain area of Arizona from the flatter cedar filled high plateau desert. We stopped to gaze at the panoramic vista before us. It stretches farther than the eye can see and is filled with canyon lands, majestic red rock bluffs, blue looking mountains, a stormy sky with rays of sun shooting through clouds making everything seem mystical and magical. While I watched her renew her spirit, I was trying to figure out how I was going to turn the Jeep around on that narrow road and head back into the forest.

It was sort of late afternoon and I knew we should start heading back. I decided that I would have to go farther down the ridge road to turn around. I could see that the road went down a steep grade and it appeared to widen enough at a curve area to turn around. Instead a pad-locked barricade blocked the road just before the turn that was out of sight until you got there.

I hate that! There should be some warning before you get into a situation. I had no other option than to turn the Jeep around at that point. The grade was too steep to back up. The situation scared me because the canyon was extremely steep and the road was covered with loose grey shale rock. It was risky but I knew that I had to do it.

I got out of the Jeep and I jumped up and down on the road and I made her do the same. I told her we needed to stretch our muscles for the ride. I also thought it a good idea to share the responsibility of what I was about to do. When the road did not give in, I felt better. I decided that the Jeep was little and the road was probably wide enough for a little Jeep.

We both got back into the Jeep and I slowly backed the Jeep. I felt much too close to the edge of that canyon. I put the gear in reverse, 4-high drive. I stopped to go forward four-feet from the edge.

It is always dramatic and frightful for the person on the down side of a cliff and that was me. There is not a door to hold me in and I can see and hear the tires go around chunking up gravel and the grass sticking up is tickling my leg. I felt smart for putting my seat belt on right before deciding to turn the Jeep around. That is exactly how it was when I saw the road under my rear tire give way. The road was collapsing. The Jeep was sliding down the edge of the canyon!

She screamed!

When she screamed, I screamed too. We screamed until our ears hurt all the time staring at each other. Finally, the Jeep stopped sliding and we laughed so hard that we cried. I was shaking because I had stood, pushing too hard on the brakes for too long.

When the Jeep came to a stop, I realized that it was good that I had a seatbelt on because we were tilted to the extreme that I would have fallen out of the Jeep and rolled down and down the canyon perhaps all the way to the streets of Cottonwood.

I prayed, "Father, tell the angels to hold us here while you tell me what to do next."

My concern was to keep us from sliding farther. My partner is bigger than I and she was on the up-side. I thought there was a good chance that her weight was holding us in balance.

My next brilliant move was to jam-force the gear into 4-wheel low and then I gunned the engine. That reaction was solely due to the fact that we were literally cliff-hanging and I wanted to move the other way, which would be upward.

It moved a couple of inches just enough to high-center the little beast on top of a boulder. I know that because it was teetering a bit. That is when I really got scared and I get this uncontrollable urge to write something down. I have done that before when having a traumatic experience, like when I got chain-sawed in the head I had to write in my own blood, that it was not his fault. I just got in the way of the saw.

I grabbed a check deposit slip and pen from the glove box and wrote:

Sorry about your Jeep. I know you like it. I had a good life. I just laughed so hard that I cried so you know I died happy. Raise the children in the Lord. Did I tell you I bought accidental life insurance for myself? This is accidental. The policy is in the drawer. I love you!

I gave it to my partner. She stuck it in her bra. I told her to start easing out her side of the Jeep. I explained that as she moved I would move her way at the same time. I reasoned with her that there was no reason for both of us to die. Besides, she would have to tell the guardian the rest of the story. I also explained that she would have to walk out, which way to go and not to worry too much because they would come looking for us. In fact, maybe sooner than later if the Jeep blows up on the way down. I should not have added that last comment because the argument started after those words.

Something strange happens when you get into big trouble with someone else. You start feeling like you are part of the other. You start being real responsible and reasonable and heroic and stupid all at the same time. My partner said that we were in this together. She would rather fall off and die with me because she did not know the way out and she would die in the wilderness anyway then added that it was the right thing for her to do.

The Jeep slipped again and that was the end of our arguing. She started moving and I did the same as fast as I could. We made it!

Side by side, we just stood there a moment staring at the predicament that I had gotten us into. The Jeep was sideways, almost lying on its side, and completely off road. The front left tire, the up-hill side tire, was off the ground. The back left tire was on the ground but barely. It was so steep. I could not see the right side of the Jeep at all.

Instead of relief, I felt angry. The Jeep just sat there and it did not move another inch. I started kicking the side trying to make it fall off the cliff. I thought it would be better for his Jeep to be at the bottom of the canyon than to try to explain how it got there, high centered on a bolder, at a180 degree tilt, just hanging. With any luck high winds would come and just blow it away. So there we were, 45 miles from any kind of help. It is getting dark, the thunderstorms are rolling in and we have no food—a problem that I knew would be high on her priority list.

I went back to the Jeep because I am finally convinced that it is not going anywhere at least not until it rains. I pulled out two light jackets, one beer, a pint of water, and 10 sunflower seeds that I found on the floor. I had a lighter in my pocket and I knew the next thing to do would be to build a fire. I asked her to do that because I needed to hike to the ridge behind us to get our exact location so that I could determine the best way to walk out the next morning. My destination was a couple of miles away and I needed to take advantage of the sunset-light.

I explained that she needed to build a big fire and that she should not be worried if I did not get back before dark because I could see a fire from a far distance and I added that I have a wilderness gift which is the ability to see in the dark. Then I left.

I felt a great relief that I was alone. I walked not even looking back. I felt free. I wanted away from her because I felt I was responsible for her safety and I did not like it.

When I reached the top of the ridge I could see the lights of Sedona. I was surprised we were that far out—forty five miles from town or any other place where we could get some help. I found out what I needed to know: that we had a long way to go, walking, and we needed to walk the same way we came in. I got a plan and felt great concern about those who would start looking for me after dark.

She made a good fire. I could see it from two miles away. I doubted that she could and felt a sense of pride for her. But as I got closer, the fire was too big and it appeared that she had done a great job at making a range fire. Parts of the dirty Jeep were shining from the fire reflection and half the hill behind her was on fire. I could see her silhouette. She was just standing there. I wondered if she even knew how hot she had made it.

"Holy-Moly!" I said out loud. "That is a big fire. I told her to make it big."

That is when I started rushing down the side of the ridge and walked right off a six-foot cliff. I am hurt. My rib is either broken or badly bruised. I also lost my prescription glasses as they flung off my head during the tumble. It was too dark to look for them.

I managed to scramble up to my feet although I also stuck my hand into a cactus while doing so. Picking stickers and stumbling down the ridge, I decided there was not much I could do about a fire a mile away but I still rushed, just more cautiously. As it grew darker, my eyes adjusted and I could see the stars through a window in the clouds. I noticed that rain clouds where moving in fast. It began to sprinkle.

As I approached the fire, I could see her more clearly. Her legs were all scratched and drips of blood had run down them. She must have scraped them while gathering sticks and grasses to make her fire. The fire was warm and she had managed to get it under control or the grass just burned out. I did not ask for details.

"You are supposed to go around the stickers and branches when gathering fire wood, not through them," I had to say.

We sat down on the dirt. I offered her the sunflower seeds to eat when she said she was hungry but she turned them down because they had been on the Jeep floor. We sipped some water but only sipped because we would need it the next day. I told her what I saw and explained where exactly we were. After that, we just sat there and did not talk for a long, long time. I did not have the heart to tell her that I hurt myself or that I was in pain. I could not lie down because I knew my body would stiffen. I felt obligated to be strong and not to whine about how I felt or talk about the circumstance I had gotten us into.

It rained a steady drizzle all night but the wet of rain seemed to miss us most of the time. That we were not drenched when morning came was something of a miracle. Both of us were anxious to start our long walk toward rescue. It was then when she heard the helicopter and she began to jump up and down waving her arms screaming, "They have come to get us! We're saved!"

Sure, miracles happen but for DPS to be searching for us in a helicopter on a Sunday morning at 5:00 a.m. after a rain storm—not very likely. Even if the guardian had organized a search during the night he did not know exactly where I was and it would be hours before anyone would even think about looking in the Woody Mountain area. I figured that we needed to save ourselves.

It was chilly and damp. To start the hike would warm us and loosen my stiff muscles. I pulled out a check deposit slip, wrote a note explaining that we would follow the main roads and as we got to cross-roads, another note will point the way. I stuck it on the windshield of the Jeep. We walked two miles to the first crossroad. I was in pain from my injury. She dawdled behind but kept within yelling distance. We did not talk much.

Along the way the incline was mostly up-hill and we came to a point where it was steeper than it had been. I knew that we were close to the mountain that the watch tower was located on. I contemplated going there but it was off-route. Rescue or traffic was more likely found in the north direction. We were tired and I told her my plan is to reach the summit and rest there. A few minutes past and she exclaimed that she was so mad at me but that she was more-mad with herself. I asked why?

"Because I took that one-pound Snicker's candy bar out of my purse before we left. I did not want to share it with you."

I laughed loudly. That hurt my side and made tears come to my eyes.

"Do you want a sunflower seed now? Or can I dig you up some worms or a tuber root and there is a good chance that I can find some grasses that are not too bitter tasting for you to munch on." I responded, though still laughing at her confession of selfishness.

It must have been about 8:00 a.m. when we stopped to rest. The forest was pretty quiet except for a couple of chattering squirrels and a few tweety-birds.

Lying down next to a big Ponderosa pine in the sun, I fell into a hard sleep.

She let me rest for about an hour before she woke me by poking me with a stick. That is when I saw the white coyote running through the trees.

"I have never seen an albino coyote before. Do you see it?" I exclaimed. "It is right over there between the acorn bush and the tree with the drop-down limb."

"No. There is nothing out there. You're delirious and obviously starving to death, seeing things."

The terrain was fairly flat on top of the ridge where we took another fork in the road. Again, writing a note on a deposit slip that said, "We went this way, watch for the white coyote."

To make a point, check deposit slips are just about the best piece of paper that you can use. There are always plenty of them. They have your name, usually your primary emergency contact person and address and telephone number printed right on them and they include nice little lines on the back to write a note.

During this trek through the woods I was dawdling behind her. I saw her running and screaming. "Help! Help!" I was thinking she had gone crazy and knew that she was wasting too much energy too soon long before I saw the truck she had managed to get stopped.

As I approached she was almost babbling, " . . . and we got stuck, and she drove the Jeep off a cliff, and we almost died, and I am hungry, and I had to walk fifty miles, and it rained all night, and I made a fire, and can you help us?" She was explaining these things as the man was gently guiding her to the side of the road to sit down.

"Do you want a burger, soup or candy bar or everything all at once?" he said as he handed her a bottle of water. He was checking out her scratched up legs too.

Our rescuers were forest service hot-shots, driving a huge water tank truck and they had rescue equipment and freeze-dried foods as standard supplies. I was still feeling guilty and refused any food but took a bottle of water.

The driver explained that he could use a radio to communicate our location and condition and circumstance to the county sheriff's office although, they were not suppose to transport civilians. I managed to explain my dilemma with the Jeep and reflected that it possibility could be a forest related danger.

"What if it falls and blows-up?" I asked him.

"Then you may have to salvage it, right? The gas tank is nearly full and that may lead to a fire in a canyon area just like the one last week that you are here to check on."

"I got your point, we probably should check it out," he said and looked at his buddy with a side glance sort of laughing at the same time.

"She will have to stay here. Ranger 2 will stay with her while you and I go."

As I jumped into the water tanker I tried to comfort her saying that I would be all right and it should not take too long to push the Jeep over the edge. I also reminded her to watch for that white coyote because he was headed in this direction.

I learned from the radio contact that a full search and county rescue party had been dispatched around 9:00 p.m. the previous night. The search party included deputy sheriffs, my guardian, my parents, kids, hunting buddies, DPS officers, in-laws and out-laws who came from miles around. That news made me feel badly for them. No one even knew that my ride-along partner was missing—that made me feel worse. No one would miss her for days.

When we arrived to the Jeep site about five miles from our rescued place, Ranger 1 whistled in a long drawn out way in response to the situation revealed. "Gosh," he said, "You two are sure lucky to be alive."

There it was, a Jeep hanging on the side of a 500 foot-plus ridge. The sight of the vehicle was slightly unbelievable from this angle because it appeared to be sitting in the air not being able to see anything holding it in position.

He explained that he has a tow chain, the tank is full of water so that its weight may enable enough traction to pull the Jeep upon the road but, he wondered if the chain would be long enough and if the road would hold and not give way under the weight of the water truck.

He did not want to try.

I explained that someday, somehow, someone would have to do it. My argument was that his truck seemed the best and safest type of equipment to try it. And, it is going to rain and rain will create an even more dangerous situation, if the Jeep stays hanging where it is. I wonder what will happen if it falls.

He said that it was against regulations and he did not want to be liable for the Jeep which was most likely going to end up at the bottom of the canyon anyway.

"Ah-ah" I said, "I will write a waiver of responsibility and I have just the thing to write it on, a check deposit slip." He laughed and agreed.

It took some doing, stress, strength, and more contemplation but he and I managed to get the chain around the back axle of the Jeep. I stood at the side as Ranger 1 made the chain taught and put the truck in low gear. Then very, very slowly he started to pull.

All of sudden, like a tree limb breaks, something gave way and the Jeep was hanging in free-airspace, swinging left to right and old beer cans and stuff tumbled out of the back and trickled down the cliff making lots of noise. The tanker slid back and the roadway started sinking under the truck's back tires.

I wanted terribly to yell, "Dive out!" but I did not. Within the next seconds I could see that the truck was gaining traction as Ranger 1 gunned the power. Then it jerked the Jeep up. It came up so abruptly it kind of jumped, then dropped and landed on top of a bolder about the same size as the Jeep itself. It was high centered, all four wheels wrapped over the sides of the rock. It looked like a Jeep-of-the-year trophy, the kind that has an object like a Jeep on top of a monumental stand. It resembled a puppy hugging a ball twice the size of itself.

Oh—oh, that cannot be good, now what? I thought and I could not help laughing.

The whole situation was a calamity and I could tell Ranger 1 was as surprised as I was. He asked, "What now?" I said, "Just hit it and go as fast as you can." When he did that, the Jeep just scraped itself off, hit the ground, popped up and landed on the road.

"Whew! Wonder if it will start? It does not really look too bad. Do you think?"

We both took a break. We breathed some extra long breaths, looked at each other, laughed and sighed and unhooked it from the tanker before we even approached the Jeep to see if it would start. When I quit shaking I climbed in, turned the key on, revved it up, put it in gear and just simply drove it up to a flat area away from that cliff.

Ranger 1 followed me back to where she waited on the side of the road with the other guy, Ranger 2 who stayed with her for comfort and in case he could intercept anyone in the search and rescue teams. No one had shown up. There was nothing else for us to do but travel home together in that tough little Jeep. The forest rangers still had to do what they had come to do, check the burn area and put out any smoking hot spots. We said goodbye and of course, our thank you statements just were not enough.

The ride home was long. We felt thankful and grateful. I was hungry and very tired. When we arrived in town I dropped her off at her apartment. We hugged and said our goodbyes and I reminded her that she could eat that whole Snicker's candy bar herself.

I finally got home and on the countertop I found a note. "If you ever get home call the Sherriff's office and tell them you are alive." I thought they should have left the phone number.

"Gosh, this is embarrassing." I said out loud to myself. I almost wished I was not alive and I knew I would feel better if that Jeep had fallen to its death. I took another deep breath, found the number and called the sheriff's office and took a tiny nap as I waited for my searchers to arrive. When they did, I realized how much trouble I had caused them. I apologized again and had to let it go as I thought about all the calamity, the new friends I made as they helped me, my friend who would probably never take another off-road trip, and how proud I was of myself for writing the notes, using my survival tactics, staying calm, planning and making it out and home safe. I also felt determined to go back and find the white coyote and I wondered if my friend would remain a friend. I must have done something right. In fact I felt as though I made a lot of good decisions and I did the right things at the right time.

Still I made some life-threatening mistakes. I also caused others to do the same to some extent. The searchers traveled in all directions north, south, east and west and one, the guardian came within one mile of us but guessed the terrain was too rough for us to be in and chose a fork in the road just 100 yards from a note that would have guided him to us.

Just remember this: You should know where you are going and tell someone who knows the country. A Jeep is a great little tough rig, dependable and probably will not let you down. You will be happy to remember to take that candy bar-sharing is a good thing. Check deposit slips make good notes, leave a trail. Walk the road before you drive down it if it is questionable. Take extra water along the next time just in case you need it. Be able to make a fire, it is your best friend and helps calm your spirit. Stay with the vehicle until you know you must not because of weather, distance, or if leaving it increases your chances of being located. Most importantly, be as smart as you are.

This will never happen again to me but something else will at another place, another calamity, another circumstance and in another situation. That is the way of the wilderness. What I learned this time may be remembered and needed the next time.

Cliff hanging in the Kaibab

Trophy Tree

It took two full day-outings, four full-grown adults that were more excited than the four children, age six to eleven tagging along to find a Christmas tree. We wanted a perfect tree because we had waited and planned for it so long. It had already been decided that the tree should be big. Bigger than any before and it had to be perfectly shaped in the Christmas tree manner.

We had a twenty foot high ceiling, an open area in the big log home where we would place it. A person could look upon the tree from the balcony loft area that topped the old hand carved-out log stairway.

There would be at least ten strands of lights circling it and we would hang the old fashioned ornaments then we would put on the silver tiny strips of ice sickles for extra sparkle. We would drink hot cocoa while we made popcorn and cranberry threaded garland and drape it over the bows; a pretty traditional plan.

The law requires a permit to cut down a Christmas tree. There is a fee for the permit and there are only two units that it is legal to cut a Christmas tree where we live. Permit applications are due in August, not a Christmas thinking time and there is a limited amount of tree permits issued. The rules are the same as drawing a permit to hunt animals and birds in our state and tree hunting can be as much of a challenge as game hunting. We had not drawn a tree permit for two years and when we received the permit to cut, the plans to hunt for a tree were discussed at length. We even took a scouting trip.

Picking out a tree in the great outdoors demands special attention to details, wide open spaces misconstrue perception because there is nothing to compare size with. On the days we went to hunt it was snowing and there was already two feet of snow on the ground, the whiteness and falling snowflakes cause one to judge size incorrectly as well.

We hiked through a square mile of forest before we found the tree, perfect in everyway. Once sawed down we quickly realized that two adults needed to lift the trunk base to drag it and another needed to lift the tree top to push it along.

We were forging away making little progress when I heard someone in the far distance scream.

"I'm pinned! I'm pinned! Hey—I said I am pinned!"

I looked at my buddy on the other side of the tree trunk and asked him to stop because I thought someone, somewhere may need our help. As we turned we heard it again, "I'm pinned!" but we could not see anyone.

Finally, we realized the guy holding up the top of the tree behind us was missing and somehow we had pulled him along instead of him pushing us along, and he was someplace under that big old tree pinned down by the branches and buried in the snow below it. That is when the thought struck my brain that the Christmas tree may be just a little too big.

The tree is much longer than the pickup truck that we dropped it next to. Even so, just like hunting, we killed the tree by cutting it down, now we have to eat it? No, we have to use it. It would be unethical to cut another even if we could find one.

It was a very hard thing to do but eventually we positioned the tree on top of the truck cab, tree trunk sticking out farther than the hood is long. We looped a rope between the truck cab top and through the side and back windows and tied it. We tied the middle portion of the tree to the truck bed area and although the tree top dragged on the ground behind we were ready to leave.

Before I climbed into the truck, I surveyed our load. You could not really see the white truck underneath it or the people inside of it chattering away. There was a little window space to look through for driving otherwise it looked like the tree was walking horizontally just above the ground, all by itself and it was talking.

Our leashing of the tree turned out to be good enough and we managed to get it home following another vehicle using his tail lights as our guide with only one more issue, a branch decided to stick its parts into the rear cab window and grabbed a kid who got poked and scratched pretty badly.

When we arrived home we stood the tree up behind the house to ready the inside. The moment the tree stood, dive-bomber pinion jays took it over for the pinion nuts in the top of it. Then a squirrel scampered up to the top of the tree to fight the jays for the nuts. It was too much; we just left them to settle their differences.

Pinion jays took over the house another day and that happened right after the flying squirrels broke the front window and knocked themselves out and flopped to the floor after they got out of their cage and flew off the loft balcony. The crazy birds fear nothing. They will dive-bomb dogs, cats and anything else that moves although, I am positive that they prefer to hit, attack and hurt human beings.

The young boy had caught these pinion jays in a live trap and took them to his room and let them go inside to see what they would do. Before I knew what was happening, all living beings and things were running about screaming, hands over heads, crashing into walls while they dodged back and forth as the birds chased them throughout.

By the time we managed to corner the five mean birds, one at a time, with a fly swatter, butterfly net and broom so that we could scoot them outside through the doors and windows we were all wounded, poked in the head mostly, we were breathing hard and we felt jittery long afterwards.

When time, we squashed the tree limbs into the tree trunk and pulled and pushed the tree into the house through a double doorway. It took four people to do it. Then we laid it down lengthwise to figure out what to do next. The tree was almost as high as the living room long. We struggled to lift it and lean it against two log walls where they make a corner. It definitely needed some support.

"I can not believe that we got that thing into the house!" he said.

"Look, we can not open or walk through the front door." I mused. "I can not see the top of the tree unless I climb to the loft!" that I did.

"It is too tall, the top is bent over," I scream down.

"It was a good thing that the kids could climb the log walls to get those anchor bolts attached so that I could tie it up."

"If it fell, it could kill somebody."

"Are you sure we got the squirrel out before we shoved it through the doors into the house? What about those jays? It hurt when that one took a dive shot and poked my head with its beak. I think it was defending its new nut tree," I said as I rubbed the top of my head. The beak wound was leaking a little.

"Sure was a good idea to use the ten gallon water tub to stand it in otherwise we would have a pitchy problem. Your second good idea was to put boulders into the tub to brace it upright."

"The tub sort of looks good, shiny bucket-silver will catch the colored lights and the presents will reflect and mirror around the outside of it," I added.

"Wonder how we are going to get the lights up there. Lets ask the kids to climb the walls again and we can pass the lights around to them on each side using that pole extension I wired together."

And so it went the rest of the day, as we tackled the Christmas tree project wholeheartedly. Eventually, it was standing perfectly straight in front of us in all its overwhelming glory.

It smelled good. The scent of pine pitch drifted through the whole house.

Stringing lights was the most difficult thing to do. The children hung onto the log walls like monkeys and two adults perched themselves onto the tops of ladders that were only half the trees' height. They had to balance themselves precariously while passing lights back and forth. Once we had circled some lights on the tree, perhaps two strands at the top, we stopped trying because it was too hard. We zigzagged the lights across the front part of the tree instead of circling around it.

We compromised decorating by throwing big clumps of silk poinsettia flowers into the top bows because even big ornaments were dwarfed to the extent that one could not see them hanging on the tree. It would have taken bags and bags of popcorn and many hours to make the garland strings so we did not do that either but we did drink hot cocoa.

The ice sickles ended up in strange designs as they were tossed onto the tree from the loft. The ceiling fan was blowing only four feet from the slightly bent over tree top and it proved to be a most helpful tool. The fan helped scatter the silver sparkling ice sickles as they were caught by the high speed wind.

The furniture would not fit into the tree's room so we stacked and squashed it against the far walls. We decided we could sit on the floor when we had the tree gathering time.

Christmas came and we did just that. It was festive and wonderful. The kids looked like little elves as they crawled under the tree to retrieve presents that had been thrown there. It is a time remembered forever because of the special Christmas tree.

That is sweet but those sweet memories faded when it came time to get rid of the tree because it had managed to dry out within the week and the pitch settled into the bottom of the trunk making it quite heavy. It would not move and it was too heavy to lift up even if there had been clearance to do so at its top. The whole thing had turned into an iron hard statue. There is only one solution and one big mess to make.

"Get the chainsaw!" he screamed.

Branch by branch we chain-sawed off. Branch by branch each one carried out. With each cut, sawdust spread all over the place and the cobwebs glistened as the dust latched on to them. We could hardly breathe even with the ceiling fans turned on turbo wind speed. The floor was not recognizable because it was covered with little sticky needles. And those needles really hurt when you step on them sock-footed.

Someone had the bright idea to burn some limbs in the big stone fireplace and that caused a chimney fire that we did not know about until we heard the fire truck sirens blaring down the street.

When the fire chief entered the house, all that he saw was a chainsaw sitting on the carpeted floor kind of camouflaged by billions of needles, next to a nearly naked tree pole, scared with circle marks caused by cutting off every limb, and the pole was still standing in a tub filled with big rocks tied to two walls with half-inch rope.

The fireplace flames had lessoned and only a cozy little smoky fire blazed by that time. The half a bucket of water I had thrown into it as the fire people were walking up the stairway had nothing to do with the special ambiance that greeted them.

The fire chief wondered if we were planning to make a Totem pole. That is also when I learned that there is a Christmas tree size limit. We had a big pole standing there with a funny needled tuff poking from the bent over top that was at least eight feet over the maximum height allowed. The chief explained further, in order to cut a real big tree, the forest service requires a special permit and they charge a higher fee. Only townships are issued those.

The firemen seemed friendly enough as they looked around and they went away once the smoke died down.

The whole matter was more pleasant than the time the game ranger came for a visit in response to a neighbor who had called to complain about the live deer I had tied up in the back yard. It was just a full sized archery deer target.

"If we untie it do you think it will run away?" I asked him.

It was probably the same person who called the fire department about our chimney fire and who called game and fish about the duck that had frozen in the pond, one that could not fly away because it was a rubber mallard duck decoy.

"You just can not save a rubber duck from drowning," I explained to the guy.

Now when we go to cut a Christmas tree we take along a twenty-foot metal tape measure and a digital camera so that we can measure a man then take a picture of that man standing in front of the tree to determine the tree's height before we chop it down.

I suppose we will never be lucky enough to get another trophy tree although, getting one in a life time is probably enough.

The Gorge

I am so hot that I feel like I am on fire burning from the tail up. My hair is so wet it is dripping sweat down my back causing steam to rise. They should have named the place flaming gorge because it is so flaming-hot.

We arrived late the night before, on a scouting trip in new lands that we have never ventured in for a very important event, four months from today. We are there to find the Desert Big Horn sheep.

This is a once-in-a-life-time hunting permit, it seems that you have to be fifty-something to even get drawn, which is a mistake because you need to be much younger to be able to handle the torture of cliff-climbing, sweating, toting equipment, falling down shale rocked ridges, running on foot over rocks and cactus for that better look, and while packing heavy stuff. The pressure is on.

There is not another type of hunt in the nation, more sought after or coveted by other hunters. Something so important, takes some preparation and scouting the territory is one of those preparing things you should do.

For the first time, we have a guide with us because it takes an expert to access the country, to find the illusive little sheep, and you need some very special kinds of gear and horses or mules to traverse the extreme landscape because you are not eighteen years old any more.

Our guide, Ernie, is much younger than I, more tenacious and excited to be with us than any hunter I have known, full of energy and information. He is wearing old, totally broke-in cowboy boots with high heels, a brown-grey plaid short sleeve light flannel shirt, and tight Wranglers. His belt buckle is really a big shiny one with his initials struck in a centered circle. He comes with a high-off the road Ford truck today, high powered binoculars, a tripod to steady the binoculars, and cheese, crackers, oysters, two cans of Vienna sausages, chocolate bars, granola bars, water, and jerky.

I knew a little about Ernie before I met him because he had taken my hunt partner on a previous guided hunt into Ely, Nevada where they had a successful mountain lion hunt, in snow with hound dogs for tracking, horses, mules, quads, and five other real special "I'll-hunt-till-I-die" guys. That guided hunt was won through a raffle drawing.

After introductions, and loading a few things into the truck we take off in a northwesterly direction. Travel through a tiny little community with a little creek flowing through it, around a mesa that must be two miles high and from what I can see, at least ten miles long and who knows how wide. I am guessing it could end at the edge of Zion National Park but I do not know if it goes that far surely, it looks like it on the maps. We are in between St. George, Utah and Mesquite, Nevada and it is a place that is very hot.

Ernie explains that we are going into the hunting unit from this direction because, "There is an old road that cuts up through the vertical side of the mesa, it is a rough ride, coiling through some canyons, the road winds around like a rattler lays ready to strike.

Well, he was pretty accurate explaining the place because as we walked up the bluff to the spotting place, I saw strange cactus, burnt from the bottom up, that left a tree trunk looking base, and they had palms fanned out in wide rubbery paddles at the tops. The paddle leaf had one big thorn sticking straight out the tip that looked like a hatching chick's egg-tooth, sharp and grabby.

Sandy loamy dirt, nothing green grows. Black rocks protrude out of the sand every so often. There are no tumble weeds or scorched grass either. Grey dirt, weird.

Ernie explains, "Big Horn sheep need very little water. There is no water up here and there is nothing that lives here except sheep because of it. They get most of their moisture from cacti."

No birds, no wind, no lizards, nothing but stupid white hunters dressed in green-brown very out-of-place camouflage clothing, heavy boots and wearing baseball type hats that match their shirts. And these stupid white hunters have very red ears being too hot to cool off.

I checked it all out and my brain took snap-shot pictures and saved them in my head. I purposed to remember because I did not know if I would ever see or experience anything similar again. Sometimes, close by places can be very foreign and so can the people you meet in those places.

I was having a great time.

Finally, we reach the top of the mesa and approach a slight depression that revealed the birthplace of a pretty significant canyon.

"Oh, thank you Lord!" A tiny breeze floats by.

We found a place to sit so that we could steady our tripods and binoculars upon them. At first, I could not see anything except dark shadows on the north side of big rock ledges. Then I spied a white spot. Almost the same instant, the other two crazy white guys saw the same spot and it moved. We got us a first time look at a big horn sheep's rear!

"They are tiny. No taller than my Labrador dog. All head, not much body, sort of colored and about the same height as a white-tailed deer but with shorter legs and big wide, over sized looking black hoofs." I declared, "That head and neck is almost one-third its total body length."

"That is a small one. It is a ewe. Ewes have shorter, smaller horns that never exceed half a curl. The one to the right is a young ram. See how the horn just starts to curl at the top of its ear? Rams never shed their horns. The rings on the horns have some indication to how old they are, measured by the thickness between the grooves and the length between the rings," Ernie explained.

"Did you hear that? He snorted. Ewes ba, and lambs bleat," Ernie whispered.

He could have talked and I could have listened all day long and I would not need to have an opinion or make a peep. By now I know that he is smart, experienced, strong, and he has keen, sharp eyes. I know because he is pointing out another ram, broader bodied, not much taller than the others, they have little ears and this one has much bigger horns and a curl in them that continues to make about a three-quarter circle around the ram's eye. This is not a trophy, but getting closer to the one we are wishing for and hoping and wanting to see. Ernie makes a knowledgeable guess; the ram is about four-years-old.

He also tells us that there are bigger ones in the area and that he has them pegged and picked out and saved for the hunt. He suggests that we get out.

"We don't want to educate them too much," he adds.

So we sneaked out and over the ridge and out-of-sight. Once done, we had a little chat and told tales of other sheep hunters and ate the oysters, crackers, cheese, drank the water, and chomped up some Hershey bars excusing our over indulgence because we did it for extra energy.

That day was my real 50th birthday, August 8th, and to celebrate we visited Mesquite, Nevada. We had a terrible dinner, met Willie Nelson and he sang "On the Road Again," and the will-be-ram-shooter danced with Willie's girl friend or wife or whoever she was. Then we rented four go-cart rides for $5 each where I got to run a young whipper-snapper into the wall two times. He deserved it because he tried, but failed to do the same to me.

The next morning we drove home to wait out the four longest months of the year to pass. Finally it is the day—day one of the Dessert Big Horn sheep hunt has arrived and starts at 4:00 a.m.

We arrived while the sun was setting the night before opening day and were able to glass-up a herd of sheep on the side of the thousand-plus high foot cliff ridge we had camped under. Ernie drove up. This time he brought another guy who is to be our camp cookie, his name was Burnt, and he looked like he was.

Burnt's hair, what was left of it, looked like it had been singed off. I know exactly how that had occurred and so do you. He had obviously been walking around in that flaming heat during August. His skin was red, his eyes a crystal clear river blue. He was aged about as much as me in years but he looked much older. He wore the same type of old high-heeled cowboy boots and boasted a grin about as wide as a sunset stretched out on the horizon. He had very white glistening teeth. His Wrangles were looser than Ernie's but his shirt was a familiar plaid in muted red and blue shades. His hand-shake was warm, firm, yet gentle and sincere. His hands were rough and used. I liked him immediately! And I mused, what a privilege it would be for him to cook for me.

I was not supposed to be along for the actual sheep hunt. It is pricy to book a ride-along on a guided hunt. Even so, Ernie liked me enough to allow me to come along. He had replied to the request with the question, "What's another biscuit?" And added, that he liked me and from our previous visit, he thought I was tough enough to make it, and a witness is always fun for storytelling later, and he had a horse named Sugarfoot, that he was sure would like me.

He explained that he and Burnt would have been there earlier but some stupid person had barricaded the road off the highway and he had to call someone to get the padlocked gate open. I mention that because there does not seem to ever be a time when things just work out as they should, perfectly.

Ernie was amazed when we showed him the sheep and commented that had never happened before. The twenty or so others before us "Could not spot a loan tree growing' on the side of a blank hill, let alone seven Big Horn sheep milling around eating a cactus over two miles away."

We jumped into the truck and drove someway for a long ways to the other side of the mountainess canyon we had woke up under where our guide had placed a truck, horse trailer, and had unloaded three of the most beautiful horses alive. They were tied up individually to bushes and loaded with saddlebags, treats in those, and a gun sling was attached to another. I knew which one was Sugarfoot: no gun sling, she was the prettiest, and she was already giving me the look, one that said, "Come-on, get-on, I'll take you." Ernie must have had a little talk with her.

Now I am really getting excited.

We traverse straight up. It was difficult to stay saddled. The horses were sure-footed and chose the way to meander between cactus, rocks, and ravines and they seemed to get a bit too close to canyon edges but did not falter.

It took a couple of hours to top-out on the mountain plateau and then we had to travel to the other side where the gorge ran through at the base of it. What a beautiful sight that is. I could touch a cloud with my right hand and at the same time see all the way through the state of Arizona where the San Francisco Peaks poke up about 400 miles away.

We each found one of those poking, rubber palm leafed things to tie and drape our reins and dismounted. My legs were a little shaky while the blood rushed through them differently than while riding. I grabbed my pack that was full of hunter stuff including water, oysters, ten crackers, eight knives, a knife sharpener, a saw, a game bag, tissue, Chap Stick, two pairs of latex gloves and some rope. The other guys would have the rest of what was needed.

We hiked and scoped and sneaked and sweated and grinned at each other and sat in precarious places hanging off cliffs for hours where we spotted and watched Big Horn sheep. I recall twenty or more in different areas and in small herds. Some alone, others had young rams, ewes, and there were a few lamb-sized. They were amazing to watch scamper around the cliff sides effortlessly. They jump astoundingly long distances across sharp, loose shale rock, to and from slippery narrow spaces. They can jump straight upward five to six feet from a dead stance. They do not seem to be bothered by our presence or the tumbling pieces of rock that make a lot of noise as they fall off and down into some other world.

We had found some pretty nice ones but the shooter and the guide knew there were older and bigger rams there, we just had not located them yet.

One of these moments the guide and shooter scaled down a hundred-foot sheer cliff to sneak around the point that was hindering the view to see if the ram spotted at over a mile away could be the One. I was guarding the gear they needed to leave behind. They were gone a long time. It was a beautiful day and it was not hot, the temperature was in the mid-sixties. When they returned they were laughing and joking and tired. We had some snacks and drinks and they described a ram they may go after, maybe on the last day.

Ernie thought that we should plan on hiking hard the next day into an area where he had located a large ram, not a major Boon and Crocket trophy but he explained, "It is a big one for this gorge strip area, it is at least a seven-year old ram and will measure nicely."

It was a beautiful ride out. The horses followed each other down canyons and we skirted the edge where we could see the deep gorge most of the way. When we arrived back at camp Burnt had prepared a delicious evening meal of chicken, corn on the cob, biscuits with honey, salad, and Dutch-oven peach cobbler with ice cream.

The next morning we found ourselves in a different area, far from the first. The terrain was similar except there was more shale rock and it was loose and the horses did not like it. They slipped more often and tired more easily because the sides we twisted through were steeper. The ride was much longer and we were headed west instead of south from where we mounted our horses.

At the top of the ridge we tied the horses to the cactus and we walked from there to the edge of another deep cut canyon. We scoped with our binoculars at every little out-break that allowed us to look across to the other ridge or down into the steep canyon. At mid day we had some oysters, cheese, Vienna sausages and crackers with hot sauce, and some deer jerky that was peppered heavily; the perfect snack.

Then we continued covering every inch of terrain that we could manage to see. We continued this way until late afternoon; we needed to start moving back toward the horses soon although, Ernie thought we should take a look off the next canyon opening that was farther ahead.

"From there you can see the highway and gage how high the cliff we are on really is. You can see the Virgin Gorge River, the town, and the beautiful colors in the canyon walls. There is nothing else like it in the world. We may not come back here."

Then he instructed us to leave the packs. We will pick them up on the way back because we are only going a little way. And off we trot to see more of the world.

We come to a cut where we can walk out onto the ledge safely and gaze. Only seconds passed when after viewing all that is around, then looking closer to the side of the cliff we are sitting on, a ram is walking under us against the cliff wall only 200 yards away. We cannot move even though the ram is walking away and his back is toward us. All that we can do is to wait motionless until he walks out of our sight then we can move into a better position.

The ram topped the horizon where a narrow game trail slipped in between twin towering bluffs that sort of arched at the top. It was a hole in the wall. As he barely entered the arch way, rays of sunlight were shining behind him, he stopped and turned and looked over his right shoulder and stared at us.

"Gosh!"

His look said, "I knew you were there. I am wise enough to get away from you. You won't see me later." Then he slowly walked through the opening and was gone.

He is a big one all right! We stared at each other and then came to life rushing to get up and try to do something smart. We found ourselves surrounded by cliff. There was no way down or around. The only way to go was back and out the same way we came in. It took us over thirty minutes to work ourselves around to where we last saw the ram and knowing the sheep habits, Ernie guided us so that we should be in front of the sheep instead of behind him when we would show ourselves again.

"There he is!" I heard the whisper.

He is under us. He is less than 250 yards away and he is moving. He looked closer but we were looking through our binoculars. The shot is at a straight down angle and under the shelve we find ourselves lurching over. The shooter turns his scope down, shoulders his rifle and I have to hold onto his belt loop and waste band to keep him from falling off the ledge. That is a real hard shot to take.

The ram comes out just to the right of us. The shooter still cannot get balance and shoot at the awkward angle.

"Wait, wait, be still, stay ready, hold on," we all had the same thoughts.

Now, in a situation like that, no one breathes. No one can breathe. No one can flinch. Everything around you reveals itself in slow-motion. Time stops. Somehow you feel every muscle in your body and they are usually hurting and pulsate. You can even feel your blood moving through your veins. That is when you know you are experiencing a very intense rare moment. And, that you might be a bit excited.

The ram moves slightly further and turns his massive head and tan-gray horns; full curl; massive base. The left horn has been broomed off.

Sometimes rams rub their horns against rocks purposefully to shorten them because as the horn curves around it can block his vision, the words run through my mind like a 50 mile an hour wind and I am still holding onto his britches, balancing on a cliff.

"Ka-Boom!" A shot fired.

The ram stumbles and falls. As his body hits the ground it slides. His head drops and the weight causes his body to slide closer and closer to the drop off that has no bottom. If it falls, it will land at the river edge, too far to see from this height.

"Oh, pray and pray hard that it will not fall off," I whispered.

Ernie moves. Again there is no way down, through or over. There is no way to go except back and around, then down the cliff to the prized animal.

He tells us to stay there and watch it while he makes it around, and he says he will do it as quickly as he can. We have to sit there and watch, helpless to do anything.

"I sure hope we do not have to watch it fall off," I said out loud, "That would be rude of him to make us do that."

As I waited for the next thing to happen, optimistically, I felt very proud and happy. I felt amazed. I just could not believe it all had happened so quickly, yet it seemed to take forever to play out. It was not at all what it was dreamt to be. It was a lot easier for one thing. Now, here we are just watching the ram slip and slip closer to the edge, tiny little inches at a time.

Then I felt remorse because the hunt was over. I wanted some dinners cooked for me, more than just one. We had planned thirteen days to hunt the Big Horn.

Ernie is taking forever.

We are mostly convinced that the ram is stuck, not sliding further although we can see that its back is slightly over the edge and if his massive head falls or slips that way again, the weight of it will pull the whole sheep over and down and gone. We want to start moving now. We think we should because the light is going to leave us soon. We know exactly where the ram lays yet it is getting very difficult to see. The sky is turning that no-color that only happens at dusk and just before sunset.

"Dang! Our packs are way back there, about a mile away, just where we left them. Oh yeah, we will be right back to pick them up," I mimic Ernie as I remember what we did.

"He's the guide, that's why we pay him, he has knives, he knows how to do this," the shooter replies.

Then finally, we can see Ernie who just made it to the cliff edge. He needed to get down the steep walls next. The sheep was hard to see from the cliff side looking down. There were too many rocks and ledges and there is too steep a decline to see it lying. It was very good that we stayed where we were on the other side so that we could guide him to the ram. Once Ernie reached the ram, we began our hike around to meet him. It was a long ways around, and rugged loose shale rock made it slippery and more difficult.

Eventually, we were leaning over the ram just admiring him from tip to tail. Ernie gets a little camera out of his pocket, sets it on his tripod and turns the mechanism to automatic picture taking mode, then jumps up with us where we pose behind the sheep.

"Click, Click." We have pictures now.

I was drawn to admire the ram more. I note that his hooves are gushy sort of rubbery to the touch and webbed looking between two cloven hooves. The hooves are sharp-edged, elastic, and concave. They are doubled-loved, 3.5 inches long. His coat is soft, not like an antelope's stiff hollow hair, more like a deer's hair or a dog's.

My hand stretched to the widest length is nine inches, this not enough to encircle the base of the horn. He has a whitish belly. His tail is short and pointy but tuffs with thin hair toward the end. He smells good. Like fresh green grass smells but there is no grass around, maybe it is more like the wetness of a cactus smell.

He is very handsome and a very magnificent animal. He is very muscular, yet sleek and smooth and streamlined. He is short probably about thirty inches high to the top of his back. He looks like he is about fifty-five inches long with his little tail. His nose is light tan almost white and it looks like he stuck his nose in dirty milk because the color of it just stops where his lips end and cheek begins.

The same whitish color is around his eyes sort of like a raccoon's bandit markings. His eyes are very large and black. Deer have big eyes but these are even larger and more mystifying because they are. He has a fat belly and his muscles are very stout and thick. His neck is almost as thick as his belly and I can see why it needs to be that strong. It is because his horns are so heavy, thick, and solid. They have weight as if they were steel or of very solid rock.

Ernie said, "The ram is probably nine-years-old and will score over 150. A score of 170 is very good—maybe record. This is one of the largest I have seen in this isolated area we are hunting in."

"He is absolutely beautiful!" I declare.

You have to appreciate and love and know the animal you hunt. You have to know that hunting is a good thing for many reasons. You have to believe that, and learn that, and conserve the country and the habitat with a passion so that these mighty animals and all others will still be walking earth after we are gone.

It looked like Ernie was starting to skin the cape area when we arrived even though he had been working on it for at least thirty minutes. It was funny because he was working very hard using a tiny little 2-inch blade pocket knife to do the job. He had not even drawn blood yet. We laughed because we were so stupid to leave every thing and more than what we needed only a mile away and realized it would only take a couple of hours to retrieve the stuff. Only, two hours we did not have.

Here we are so prepared to be so unprepared again.

Ernie was concerned because the horses were even farther, over two miles away and it was rough terrain in between us and the horses. And he explained that horses can not come the way we did because they can not walk on the sides of steep cliffs through shale rock so, he would have to walk his horse in from the top of the ridges we walked around and through the cuts.

It was almost dark and we absolutely had to get the ram up the cliff, pack it out, and ride out that night. I do not know if we really had any other options, like stay there or wait for people. I suppose the urgency could have been a matter of hungry horses or late for dinner or that it would be boring to do anything different.

"My horse will pack the ram. The other horses do not do that. I need to go get him and bring him to the top of the ledge over there," as he pointed upward toward the first tiny star twinkling in the northern sky. "Do you think you can get the ram to the top?"

Sure, the shooter nodded in agreement, after all we are practiced and true hunters. Ernie handed the shooter the tiny pocket knife and off he went to get his horse.

Shooter took the knife, stared at it as he twirled it between his index finger and thumb, shaking his head, with arched eyebrows and said, "This will be a first."

Ernie yelled back as he topped the cliff, "I'll pick up the packs and gear on the way back."

The shooter and I went to work and pulled and stabbed and grabbed and jerked and did very little cutting. Eventually, we got the cape off and trophy ready for the shooter to pack out. I strapped my outer-layer long sleeve T-shirt over my shoulder making a pack-sling to carry quarters of meat and then I stuffed the tender loins and back straps into my cargo type side pockets that go from the hip to the knee until my pants were so tight and bulging out the sides that my legs would barely bend. That caused some problem as I tried to scale the cliffs to the top. I decided that the meat was being tenderized as I climbed, probably making it better.

When we both finally reached the top, we collapsed to rest. Climbing out with our treasures had been the most difficult thing to do so far. We looked at each other and laughed again and said things to each other like: What a hunt. What a nice shot you made. That is a really big—Big Horn sheep. That tiny knife has to be some kind of record skinning, cleaning tool. Why did we do that, leave our packs? We have state-of-the-art knives somewhere out there and they are sharp. Where is Ernie? Our prayers were answered when that ram did not fall off that cliff. What did we hire a guide for? Will we get a refund because it only took two days and we had to do the hard part? Ernie sure knows the country and the horses are great. Wonder what Burnt is fixing for dinner?

When we felt like it, we started walking toward the place where Ernie was to meet us and eventually, we intercepted. Ernie had retrieved our packs and had tied his horse in a safe place on top of the ridge. When he reached us, he really laughed at the tender loins hanging from my pockets. Then he took some of the load and we helped him when we reached his horse, load our ram evenly on both of its sides. The horse did not seem to really like the ram being placed upon him. He glared at it and snorted and side stepped then he was just fine. I guessed he just needed to complain a little.

Once we were ready we started the hike back to the other two horses, Ernie walking and guiding his horse in front. It was dark but we could see the ground and the stars and a big bright moon had risen to the seven o'clock place in the sky. It took some time, I think over an hour to reach our rides.

We mounted our horses and I admit it was hard to get on Sugarfoot. My leg had a difficult time swinging over but the hardest thing was to leap upward and pull myself into the saddle. My muscles did not want to function. The shooter led his horse to the side of a big rock and then got on, something I would do if I have to do it again.

I was concerned because Ernie was going to have to walk himself and his horse out all the way and we were 8 miles from the truck and trailers. We progressed and Ernie was leading us a way that we had not gone before. We were on the edge of the mountains' ridge that we camped under—way under. I recognized the top of the place where the sheep live just lower, that we watched the first day butting heads over cactus juice.

I could see vehicles that looked like ants traveling on the highway way below. I could see flashing headlights were I thought our camp may be and sure enough, Ernie said that it was Burnt signaling us that dinner was ready, or that he could come save us if need be. Ernie pulled a tiny flashlight from his pocket and signaled back to Burnt.

"Does not Ernie carry anything full-sized hunter-style?" I asked the shooter and we laughed. We decided that he could have a passel of tiny little hunt-things in those pockets because he must only have miniature versions.

Burnt must have spied the two long and two short flashes that Ernie sent because he signaled back the same sequence. Then the headlights turned off and we circled around the last point on the mountain then we saw a deep cliff-sided gorge that we obviously were going down.

We went around and over and through and over and down and up. Riding a horse was quite an adventure through it. My horse leaned so much forward as she traversed the steep down grade that I was lying my back on her rear-end with my feet next to her ears one moment then, I would be lying right up on her head breathing heavily in her ear with my feet up on her rear going up the other side. When I was not tilted too and froe then I was leaning right or left to the extremes that I felt I was sitting on the side of her belly. I was sliding in the saddle so much that I believed I would rub the stitches loose on my pants. My legs hurt just from balancing my body one way or the other.

Shooter, who was riding behind me, was struggling as well. Every so often, he would growl then say something inaudible. I could tell he was not having a pleasant conversation with his horse.

I thought this is the best day of my life. Never could I have imagined this adventure and the uniqueness of it.

Meanwhile poor Ernie on foot is leading his horse and us through the most impossible cactus brush, rocky, dippy, sandy, rough, scratchy, lonesome area I have ever felt. Ernie was walking at a fast pace and I thought I saw his boots smoking from the wear-out they were getting and his feet must have been hurting real bad. We had already traversed four miles, I was positive, and we had a lot farther to go because we were still very high in that canyon and our destination was a pretty flattened out place.

I looked at the starry, beautiful, clear sky and at the moon which had risen to the nine o'clock place.

It had gotten a whole lot darker in that canyon and it was difficult to tell where the cliffs were or where the supposed trail should be. There were big tree cactus things that loomed out like skeletons wearing sombreros. Those had to be the same cacti that looked burned and had the palmed out tops but they sure looked different in this place, in the dark, standing on the cliffs, and jumping up in front of you. My horse slightly dodged them and forgot that I was riding her because she shoved my legs into the sides of the trunks. It hurt, they were hard and roughed-up and grabby.

Well, she sure was a Sugarfoot because she had managed not to walk off a cliff or slip or stumble. I felt lucky to be riding her. On the other hand, the horse Shooter was riding behind me kept running into me and Sugarfoot and I could tell that horse did not like his rider and seemed to be trying to knock him off. The horse even reared up one time but it was a little rear in that his front hooves only came up together, ten inches or so. When that happened, I thought it found a snake but Ernie says there are no snakes; there is nothing alive, only stupid white hunters. The horse probably jumped when he got too close to the edge, "Scared himself," Ernie said.

Shooter tightened his grip, sat taller, scooted is rear center in the saddle and adjusted his toes in his stirrups. I wondered if he had been sleeping because it looked as though he had just tuned-in. How does one do that? I asked myself.

Well that was quite a ride; one that can never be duplicated or enjoyed as much by me. The air was warm, clear, and I truly could have grabbed a handful of stars with one hand and hold on for dear life with the other while I watched the moon make its way to the ten o'clock place. I did not care if I ever arrived to my destination—where ever that was.

Ernie was still hoofing it. He had not stopped, not one time to breathe, rest, or drink water. He was hiking at such a pace my horse could not keep up. Ernie would disappear for a moment at the bottom of the gorge and reappear on the other side coming out of it. I do not think a horse can track by smelling but on the other hand, it did not seem to matter where Ernie actually was, in sight or out of sight, our horses seemed to sniff and track and put their hoofs exactly in Ernie's foot prints.

Another thirty minutes passed and we came to the last rise, looking down we saw headlights and a shadow of a man walking around.

Ernie yelled, "Burnt here we are and we have a trophy!"

Ernie lead his horse to the back of the horse trailer and gently started to unload the ram and gear, then the pack and the other tack and lead his horse to water and gave him a handful of oats and rubbed his neck and nose and spoke soft words to him before he stopped to talk to Burnt or us or to take a little break. I admired him for doing that because it was obvious that he appreciated and loved that horse. It was cherished. He and Burnt helped Shooter and I do the same for our horses. Then they loaded them into their places and we took off for camp.

I do not remember exactly what we ate late that night; I think it was roast beef and pot-baked potatoes and carrots and biscuits with gravy. It was very good, even though saved for hours, it was Dutch-oven hot and prepared perfectly.

I slept so contentedly.

The next morning was not eventful; we slept until daylight, packed, ate some pancakes, eggs and sausage then drove home. Burnt's morning camp coffee was so good, hickory I think.

It is law in Arizona to officially register Big Horn sheep when taken. To do this proper, takes about an hour and two officials do it together. Score is determined by many individual horn measurements.

When the scoring is finished, the official score and shooter's name are recorded and a tiny little hole is drilled in the back-base of one horn where a little metal cylinder-shaped marker with an engraved number is permanently placed. They do scientific studies using the minute amount of powder taken from the horn. Studies show things like moisture content of the land, the sheep's growth rate, health, age, and many more things that help manage conservation for the magnificent Big Horn sheep and the habitat they live in.

This Big Horn sheep scored 153.28. It was about nine years old. A ram's lifespan is 10 to 15 years when habitat is good. The expert said that our ram is a "very sweet trophy" for the unit it lived in.

Big Horn Sheep, Ernie Hafen, Netter and Rick Lawrence

Pike

Thirty seven years ago Lake Mary held many, large Northern Pike. Pike are ugly, prehistoric in appearance, very strong pound for pound and they are an aggressive fish. They are extremely slimy, covered in heavy glop that oozes off the fish skin. The glop looks and feels worse than dirty heavy black oil and it sticks to your fingers and smears your cloths and it is hard to rid the smell of it. They have razor sharp teeth in a head that is one-third the body's length. Believe it or not, they taste pretty good in spite of their looks and habitat—black lake mud.

They are bottom dwellers and are carnivorous, eating smaller fish mostly. They are fighters as they are pulled closer to the surface. At first when hooked, they feel sluggish and they roll making the angler think they have snagged something on the lake bottom or that he has caught a blogged underwater branch. So, there is a surprise element involved in actually catching a big one.

The fishing rig most successful for us includes a heavy pole, ten inch wire leader, extra weight and some type of big lure such as a diving Rapallo or what I call, a whore lure—one that has a spinner above the hook part and a whorish looking skirt that is squiggly because it drapes back two-inch rubber band sized multicolored streamers that hide the hooks. It takes some kind of action lure to wake the Pike and get them interested, I think.

Lake Mary is only about a twenty-minute drive from home and because it is not far, we often went fishing late afternoon. On this day, we arrived on the lakeshore just as it started to rain lightly. That was alright because we carry rain gear, poncho type. Rain can be good or bad for fishing it just depends upon the fish's mood.

Our ride-along, Mark, was a long-time friend, a good sport, athletic, tall, handsome, smart, humorous, talented, an entertainer by nature who we had talked into coming along just for laughs. I would have to call him a rookie because he did not know how to fish, not really. He did not know what to expect because he had only caught tiny bluegill as a kid. I desired extra entertainment that day even though I did not have his best interests at heart.

Because we helped Mark rig his pole, he was first at getting his line into the water and before he could even get comfortable, a fish grabbed his whore lure and jerked the pole off the stack of rocks he had sat it on temporarily while getting a drink and stool set up. He grabbed the pole and started reeling in sort of off balanced, stumbling over rocks, pulling the pole up and down and swinging it side to side like he saw them do on TV fishing shows. He was excited too, yelling at us and at the same time talking to his fish still in the water.

"I got you, I got you! Come here. Quit it, you're goin' to pull me in. Stop it, you're hurting me! How big are you? What are you?" saying things like that.

After about an eight minute show, the fish surfaced and jumped and twirled around. This scared Mark so much that he threw his pole away and as it hit the ground the fish was pulling it away into the water. Mark was screaming and huffing and running with flaying arms as fast as he could the other way toward higher ground and the safety of the truck.

Mark's actions and reactions took some intervention. The pole Mark was using was one of our good poles and it had a fairly new reel mounted to it along with that five dollar whore lure tied to the line. There is no way it was going to be pulled into the depths of Lake Mary by a fish. My other buddy, fast as lightening, got to the pole and being the expert he is, pulled any slack out of the line to make sure the fish was still on the other end. Then, we commenced to talk Mark into coming back and finishing the job he had started. He was willing but very leery.

As the fish approached the shore and it became visible, Mark got scared of it again. He was shaking and it was not from the wet, he truly wanted to throw it away.

A baby would just look at it, run or howl, with lips quivering as he looks for an adult in hopes of urgent rescue. Mark looked just like that baby.

"Trust me. Pike are a frightful sight and they can hurt you! They make monsters in horror movies look tame. It is a natural reaction to run away from them and the realization that you actually worked to catch one on purpose is just as overwhelming," I said while I laughed, but it was in sympathy.

Mark managed to get his pocket knife out of his pocket and opened it with one hand while still holding and tugging the fishing pole. He was going to simply cut the line and let the fish swim away. He absolutely did not want that fish any closer to him and was going to take control. I guess he had enough.

We were both standing right next to Mark and took away his knife. We made him do it. He reeled the fish in by himself. Then I took over the job of getting the fish off the hook because my other buddy's pole was jerking and line escaping as another big hefty pike struck it.

I used heavy groves, pliers, and stood on the pike's tail as I worked the whore-lure out of its mouth. The teeth were sharp and they gnawed at the pliers. I could hear them grind against the pliers metal. Once freed, I stuck a stringer hook through its gill and mouth, careful not to touch the nasty thing's slime or head. Quite a masterful process, I thought.

After the fish was all put away, so to speak, Mark felt like fishing some more with the condition that he would pay me 50 cents to take the hook out of each fish he caught, and he handed me the first 50 cents right then to convince me he was serious.

I made five dollars and 50 cents in about an hour while I caught my own pike. Of course, the money was not the reward. I had to take it in honor. I chuckled and felt delighted every time he caught another and when he needed to traded me four quarters for a dollar bill.

We continued to fish and each of us caught our limit before dark. The best part is that the three of us continued to have a wonderful summer playing, laughing, and fishing together after that pike initiation.

During that same summer, I caught a monster rainbow trout on a Marshmallow that I sprinkled with garlic salt, out of Marshall Lake in the rain while sitting on a collapsed cardboard box with an old rag blanket over my bare legs, studying Henry Thoreau's, *On Walden Pond*, for a college exam.

That rainbow trout weighted five and one-half pounds. It is unofficially known as the largest rainbow pulled out of that little mountain marshy pond-sized lake. That was a surprise. I also thought the happening a bit ironic because of what I was reading and where I was.

By the way, I got my picture taken holding that trout at Ruff's. I also think that I may have invented original power bait that year. Too bad I did not think to perfect it for today's market. If I had, perhaps I would be fishing more often.

Lake Mary, five miles from Flagstaff, Arizona

More Bucks

I have not been what I would consider a successful deer hunter although I have hunted deer more often than any other big game animal and have bagged a few bucks along the way.

We had knocked open the woods' doors before sunrise for three mornings. The unit offered another rugged area, meaning an area with deep canyons and steep gullies. It is never easy.

The only good things about it was once I hiked to the top, I could sit on some bluff and use binoculars to spot and find deer and other animals to entertain me through the morning hours. After that time was spent, it was always a down hill hike back.

The next day we went all the way to the Camp Verde area and worked ourselves back up the north canyon area riding on an old road that my Granddad called, the old Blue Grade Highway but I can not find that name on a map. It may have been called that in the olden days because to this day the road has a surface of blue grey shale rock and it slopes at an extreme grade as it climbs to the mountains' rim.

The road is part of the original trail that eventually ends up on top of the west part of the Mogollon Rim and you can get to the Apache Maid area, about eight miles farther from where it tops out. The route is more than 100 years old pioneered around 1873 by General George Crook while he was the U.S. Army commander in Arizona.

The Mogollon Rim has an average height of 7,000 feet although we stopped on a lower rim break and hiked back in, to a steep bluff to glass using our binoculars. After some time, we spotted a whitetail deer. It was a very big buck, five points on each side.

Again, I could not get a clear shot. My partner was closer and in range. He lifted his gun into position and got the deer in his scope. In the same instant, the deer literally jumped up out of head high brush, stretching out his front and hind legs as he leaped over a barbed wire fence.

"Kaa-boom," a shot fired.

My partner had shot the deer in mid air, in flight. It collapsed its legs while airborne like a bird will fold its wings, and fell dead to the ground.

My partner has shot at least 100 ducks on the wing, flying at high speed and while doing that, he had gained the skill to lead and shoot simultaneously, a tactic that even works on leaping deer. Imagine that.

Another hunt, a different year, basically the same area but much lower in elevation and we had walked miles with no luck in finding the elusive deer buck. It was unusual in that it was legal to choose either a black tailed mule deer or white tailed deer that season. These two Arizona species are very different in size and appearance. Each species usually live in different types of habitat at different elevations and are rarely using the same areas, although today was different.

We were just approaching another look-off place and only twelve feet in front of us, a white tailed deer and a black tailed mule deer had just reached the top and popped up in front of us. They were so close, they scared us and we them. Both bucks were very nice, very large bucks.

"Oh my goodness," I exclaimed, "Which one to shoot?"

"Kaa-boom," a shot fired and a celebration was soon to follow.

It was not me that shot. I must have been too shocked in my boots to shoot.

He chose the mule deer which in my estimation was a smaller prize than the whitetail would have been. Whitetail deer are rare and hard to find up here where we live and that one was no doubt a trophy size.

"Why in the world were they together?" I asked.

"I did not even see the other one, until he ran away. I knew the one I aimed at and shot was a beauty. I reacted on instinct, as usual," he said.

"We are in mountain lion country and a lion had them on the run. There is no other reason why both the bucks would be in exactly the same place at the same moment. What is weird, is that we were here and I was ready." he philosophically explained.

"Why did not you shoot?" He asked.

"You were slightly in front of me moving to the left gaining aim. To your left was where my deer stood for an instant. Even if I had been ready and using my natural instincts, I could not have shot with you in that place." I explained and sort of tried to laugh about it.

Then another season chasing deer I found myself in the coxcombs in the Kaibab National Forest. The coxcombs are a land formation caused by a volcanic eruption that causes hill-like land masses to protrude from a very flat area. These masses usually form a line along the terrain and are most commonly formed closely to but separate from a ridge or high mesa. Coxcombs are strange looking because they slant on the horizon in a way that makes a human feel off balanced. It is similar to a magic trick when a mirrored surface is sharply tilted and the objects sitting on top of it are not. The sight of them, and walking upon them does something to vertigo.

We had been hunting and camping for the first few days of a seven day hunt with very unhappy people. Most of the time we could deal with that although, we found ourselves leaving earlier and staying out longer than usual especially during the evening hunt.

It was the time of no-color, when all things turn grey-shadowy back and white muting together, leaving no definition or contrast between things.

I see a deer up ahead, about a quarter of a mile away and I can tell that it is a buck, the last sun shining at its back side. I get out of the vehicle, walk to the other side of the road to where it is legal and safer to shoot from, and then move to where I am about 275 yards away from the deer. I find the deer in my scope take aim and gently pull the trigger.

"Kaa-boom," shot sounded.

Deer fell, easy shot, nice shot, no calamities or problems. We can even drive right up to it and finish the chore of packing it.

"Wow! That is a first." I declared.

I walked up to my deer and my heart fell. It had no more than 4-inch antlers with cute little two-forked points on each side about as long as my index finger. They will make good steak knife handles or the perfect Jack-A-Lope—they would fit a jackrabbit perfectly, giving one antlers.

Oh well.

That sunset light was very tricky that night; throwing light, weight, height, and some kind of glory on the deer's head and antlers, sort of halo-like, as I recall.

And yet another time, that played out close to Tucson on Mount Henry. The event happened so fast that I can not remember which hunt day it was; could have been day one, when I got the first opportunity to see a deer in my scope.

I had a new partner that day, one that grew up in the area. He is famed for successful dear hunting among other things. He was hunting with me because another person was hunting with my usual partner in a canyon area in the opposite direction.

Out of the truck and straight up an extremely steep mountain became my first quest of the day. It was difficult. I was out of breath. I had to carry my gun in my hands in front of me because it was such a steep incline. It took about forty-five minutes to reach the first pointed top and from there we would decline through a cut and climb up the next higher and steeper point. I was a little overwhelmed at the energy I needed to expend.

I made it to a sit-down resting spot. My day partner glassed the area and it only took a couple of minutes for him to spot two white-tailed bucks sparring in a little mountain cut about 450 yards away. That is a long shot for me. I am most practiced between 200 to 350 yards mostly because the country I usually hunt in, does not allow the visual yardage, too thick with trees and brush.

We snuck about 50 yards closer, stopping at a bolder that I set my rifle on top of for a steady rest. He had determined that the buck on the left was the larger of the two so, that would be the one to take.

As I took aim, my partner was using a range finder and explaining that I would need to compensate for the wind, a five-inch adjustment to the left from center crosshair. Also, I needed to shoot slightly high, about 3 inches because of the distance and the downhill angle.

"Kaa-boom," I fired.

I hit low and in front of the deer and missed although, the deer did not react to the bullet blast or small puff of dirt the bullet caused. They continued sparring. I immediately knew that I needed to adjust higher, to the top of his back over the target area and hold extremely steady, to concentrate so that I would not pull or jerk the trigger, and not over anticipate the gun blast.

"Kaa-boom," second shot taken.

The deer dropped so hard or the ground was so soft that dust smoked up around it. We had to wait for the dust to settle just to make sure it was still there. The other deer were just standing there looking up toward us but they obviously could not see us in our camouflaged desert clothing or make our silhouettes out because we were sitting behind big rocks, under the horizon.

"Wow! That was fun! I want to shoot the other one. He is just standing there, I bet you that I can hit him the first shot. Can I do it? They are so little, we need two to eat." I said very sincerely, but of course I could not do that.

That was actually the very first deer that I had ever shot. My partner did not know about the jig-dance that always follows, and he looked at me very strangely as I stood to do it, and jiggle all over ending it with a loud hoot. I was thrilled.

The buck was a nice two by three, as defined in Arizona. That means he had three points on one side and two on the other, not including his 3 inch antler eye guards. Easterners would call him a 7 point, counting each little point sticking up from the main antler beam individually.

It took thirty minutes to reach the buck because we had to make the decent so cautiously avoiding cacti, loose rock, and rattlesnakes that may be slithering about.

The dressing out chore of the deer was simple because it was so small. It only weighed about 70 pounds and my partner could easily carry it out on his shoulders. I planned to carry the rifles and extra gear.

It was hard for my hunt partner to carry the deer out because he was obligated to carry and not drag because I insisted that I wanted a full mount to stand in the corner of my living room. I convinced him that I would not change my mind.

Poor guy, he fell on cactus, hurt his back and poked his leg. I scratched his gun stock when I tumbled, and he lost his knife on the return journey as well.

We were back at the truck at 10:00 a.m. and spent the next six hours waiting for the other two hunters to return. When they did, my usual hunting partner had shot a nice buck on the run. He actually shot him in the leg first, hitting low from a range of 450 yards. What a shot. Adjusting for wind and yardage, his second shot was naturally exact.

We were on the northwest border of Arizona, deer hunting. This trip was limited to five days because my bull elk hunt opened the morning of the sixth day and that was to be done on the south rim of the Grand Canyon. We would have to travel. I had already made the return trip one time because in between hunts we wrote my college term paper about what we thought of politics and Ronald Reagan, who was our U.S. President. I had to take the assignment to Flagstaff and drove back.

It had snowed during the week before. On the night before day three, it snowed again, two feet. We woke to a winter wonderland including three foot ice cycles that hung off the edges of the sheepherder's tent we were living in.

Thankful for the wood burning stove inside the tent, that also kept us warm and cozy during the night we casually drank some coffee and had a bite of bacon before we ventured out into the white wilderness. Besides, it was still snowing and in a storm like that, you really need to wait until light so that you can mark your bearings, see landmarks, and track deer who have been meandering through the snow all night.

The morning jaunt around did not produce any targets so we decided to drive around and try to cut-off fresh track. About an hour had passed before we spied a deer, about 200 yards away, a sweet buck, thick based, big bodied, four-by-four standing in the middle of the snowy covered road just looking at us as we approached him.

I jumped out of the truck, sat on my rear, stuck my elbows between my knees, raised the rifle, found the deer in my sights, clicked off safety and then he said, "Would you look at that huge rogue buck standing on the side of the sloping ridge, about 500 yards away!"

"Not again," I said as I took my eyes off my target and looked up the ridge to my left. Stupid is just stupid and I knew I was acting that way, right then.

I was amazed. The buck he pointed out was truly the largest I have ever seen. It was nearly elk size; just a giant of a deer in his prime. It was a six by six or five by six, anyway it was a record book or very close to it.

As I ogled at that buck, partner was grabbing his rifle and hat and gloves and pack and range finder and tripod and binoculars and throwing them about his body, ready to move, fast.

Believe it or not, I did not have a shot at that big one or I would have taken it. From the place I was sitting, just about to shoot the other one, partner was in the way and the angle to the big deer too far back and around from my position. I needed to move and move fast. While trying to do that, my partner was already scampering up the ridge, gaining yardage and the buck was moving straight up and away at a nice pace, faster than man can climb.

"Shucks," I said, wishing that I had shot my buck. My reason was noble: I did not want to ruin his chances of hunting and gaining the One, in-his-life-time.

I got back into the truck and the plan was for me to drive around, about a 15 mile distance following the road that cut through the canyon to the top of the mesa that he would be on, hunting that buck. He would naturally end up on the road where I would pick him up and we would go back together to pack the deer out if he got his chance.

He pushed that buck right in front of two other hunters who were working the mesa ridgeline. One of them shot the giant.

Neither of us took a deer that hunt. I chose not to shoot another little one that I had opportunity to get, it just was not in my dreams that day and I would have another adventure starting in a few hours in another place.

The most terrible deer hunt I have ever been on happened in the canyon area the other side of Apache Maid.

On the second day of the hunt, after perching on the ledge of a significant canyon all morning, it was time to leave and go back to camp. The other two hunters and I had spaced ourselves along the canyon about a mile apart and we had radio contact, timed every two hours on the hour, to check in with each other and report what we had found.

This is a usual set-up and one that we have used successfully because one hunter may spot the game moving toward another. This plan also enables hunters to gage the number and the quality of the animals living in the area.

The long way to my perching place that day was about a mile hike. A shortcut would be to climb out and over the twenty-five foot bluff just behind me. I had decided to do that.

To prepare for the short climb, I slung my gun over my head, strap across my chest and over my shoulder so that it would be tight and stable. I had put loose gear like my binoculars and radio into the pack then secured the straps and zippers on it so that my hands would be free. And up I went.

It was easy because there was a cut in the side, wide enough to work through with good hand grips and places to put my feet as I climbed. About halfway up, I heard a very strange noise—something was rumbling—and the sound was getting louder and it was coming toward me.

I knew in an instant that my partner had kicked off a rock. He just had to get me excited and sometimes he feels like I need a little joke.

Then I saw it. A giant bolder was sliding down the same cut I was wedged into. I immediately squished up into the craves as tightly as I could, ducked my head under a slight overhang hoping the rock would slide sort of over and away from my body. I twisted sort of leaning back against the side, trying to also protect my rifle because if the rock caught my rifle, the way it strapped onto me, it would have pulled me out and down. I managed to position myself in this manner within a couple of seconds, instinct and physical reaction to danger helped in doing it.

Good grief, I was in trouble and I had no way out of it.

The rock came. It scraped over my head pulling out some hair. The weight pushed and slung me against my back and into the too little crack. The weight of the rock came down hard when it hit my left hip, then it cramped and whammed my left knee where it rested for a long time, I think about ten minutes because I had some thinking time to wonder what to do about it.

I was really pinned. I could not twist or turn or reach to get into my back pack. There was no way I would be able to get the radio and the others would think I was just late or that I had taken the long way around or that I was just doodling around. I did not think they could find me if I passed out from shock or injury because I was quite hidden at this point.

I thought that the light weight metal braces on the backpack probably saved me from some worse injury. I had already concluded that I was injured some place but was not sure exactly which part would be the worst. My rifle was good, it was not damaged and I found some relief in that. I thought about how much I really like that 243, hand grip stocked gun. Then my mind went back to the boulder still sitting on top of my body and that it was difficult to breathe and that my knee and hip felt numb. That could not be a good sign.

I pushed as hard as I could and that was greater than ever before because the adrenalin was pumping and I could feel it. The boulder did not give an inch, how could it? It was about as big as sea chest, one too big for one person to move by himself; the kind of ice chest that is put at the stern of a big boat. In other words, this rock sitting on me was at least two feet thick on four sides and four feet long. Only my head, shoulders and half my chest area were not covered by its mass. I could push against it with my body and my arms but that was because it tilted just enough for me to work the arms out while it sat on my lower body area.

I pushed again and I just started praying: "Dear Lord, Father, please send your angels to do my bidding and lift this sucker off of me. Or, you could knock my partner in the head and give him the Word of Knowledge and Your divine guidance to come save me, right now!"

No kidding, the rock started slipping off of me and away. It really did feel like it was being lifted away. It was miraculous and I was one very, very thankful human being.

At that moment, I needed to move and move fast while my lower extremities were numb and the adrenalin rushing. That is what I did and when I topped out, the quad—my rescue vehicle was in sight. As the other two hunters approached they thought I was taking a nap in the sun while lying back upon it with my legs propped on the handlebars.

Lying there, I was wondering how many people have actually seen a tree fall down in the forest. The incident was a fluke, not something normal at least not something I had ever heard of happening before but on the other hand, you know that rocks break off and slide all the time and big trees fall down.

We got to camp and assessed the damage. There was definitely something terribly wrong with the knee. It was very swollen, discolored and spongy to the touch. One of the others wrapped it in ice and with an ace bandage and told me not to move as they gave me some camp medicine, and they gave me lots of it.

I continued to hunt deer, from the quad for the rest of the seven day hunt. A doe and two fawns walked right up to the quad and sniffed it and snorted at it while I was watching from a bush close by. That was interesting. The other guys had made a sort of crutch out of a cedar limb and that helped. I did not see anything to shoot but the country was gorgeous.

At least I did not wreck the hunt for the others by making them take me in to a hospital. I had decided that there was not much to be done to the knee so swollen, even if they had rushed me home. Besides, I can rest, take camp medicine, ride around, eat, sleep, and play just as well out in the wilderness. Fact is the nicest type of people and comrades are right there close, to give me that little helping pull-up to the feet when I needed to move around.

Six months later, when there are no hunting seasons I had doctors repair some torn and chipped parts inside the knee. Later I found the hip had been damaged, probably fractured but hips are pretty much self-rehabilitating. I also have gained the tendency to walk around the longer way, just to take in more scenery.

We returned to the Tucson area, the Rincon Mountains to hunt whitetail again. There we met four other hunters and we camped together. The area is large and fairly accessible although, we had to split up into pairs to hunt different areas because there were too many of us.

I chose my usual favorite partner to hunt with especially because we hunt the same, know what the other will and will not do, we have the same walking and working rhythms, and we like each others company. We both have had a few bad experiences with hunters who are not as safe or savvy and sometimes not even nice to be around so, we do not take chances unnecessarily.

We worked the area for the first twenty-four hours of hunting time and found one place that we particularly liked. We had a view from a high place on a ridge, one that the sun was at your back in the morning and it disappeared on the other side of the highest mountain range by two o'clock in the afternoon, perfect hunting conditions.

And best, we watched bucks working the draw while we were working up a hunting strategically. We knew where the deer had been, where they were going, what time they moved, where they bedded, what they ate, and where they watered by this time.

During the afternoon hunt we perched up on our bench and waited while we glassed and scoped every shadow under every mesquite and Palo Verde tree, we watch lizards and birds and even spotted a male coatimondi.

Coatimondi look to me like monkeys with longish arms and they have a very long tail but in fact they are related to the raccoon. They are active during the day and they are hilarious to watch because they are curious, noisy, and they talk to each other all the time making all kinds of sounds and screams.

Female and young coatimondi hang-out in bands of 5 to 40, and they do swing and climb around in trees. They look odd because they have a long and slender snout that I think is similar to an anteater's. Coatimondi probably do eat ants because they are known to eat fruits, eggs, seeds, insects and small animals like mice and lizards. The males are solitary loaners and a male is darker in color. He walks around with his two-foot ringed tail sticking straight up in the air.

One of our camp buddies is a biologist and told us all about the coatimondi. I had never seen one before that day and I was fascinated.

While I watched the male coatimondi stroll out of sight my partner picked up a pair of whitetail bucks coming out of the heavy brush, bedding area to our right. We quickly got into position and waited until they were in range. Meanwhile, we planned the double shot: I would take the one in front and he would take the one following simply because mine would come out first and walk into an opening. I would wait until the other showed and we would shoot at the same time; perfect plan, right?

"I'll count, on 3 shoot," I said.

"Here they come. One, two, three."

"Kaa-boom-boom!"

What a sight, two deer down but mine got up and ran away.

"Geez!" I said.

"Shoot again, there he is!" I heard him say.

"Kaa-boom," I shot again and this time he did not run away.

I could not believe it but we got them both. His was a little bigger, wider, and had thicker based antlers. But that sure did not matter to either of us.

We were so happy as we made our way down to our prizes.

We found his first and did our jig. Then we found mine and did another jig and then the real work started. I thought I was going to die my tenth time, trying to get those deer out of there. It was so tough that the work drew the last bit of strength from our souls. I am not sure how we managed. You might wonder why we did not go for help. It was too far and the others were hunting and we had the time and guts to do it.

Well, the truth is that it did not work out that way, exactly. My partner did get his deer, a 400 yard shot using the 7-Mag which has much longer range than my 243 caliber. My deer did run away as I said although, Partner shot when I called number two and his shot scared mine away. I did not shoot that day because that deer was too far away.

The next morning we returned because we knew the second buck stayed in the area. We spotted him right away. He was feeding on the side of the far mountain side slope, not too far away although to get into shooting range, we had to drop off the bluff, work around a hill, cross a gully, and climb while keeping the breeze in our faces and staying out of sight as we moved through the country. The deer started moving off the side of the slope and heading into lower country. We were able to see him every few minutes and made the plan to cut him off over the next rolling desert rise.

We snuck over, at low profile and squished our bodies down to avoid standing out on the horizon to glass him and determine exactly where and what to do next. There he was, just coming up from a shallow gully, when he got on top of the rise he would be about 350 yards away.

I sat down fast. Partner handed me a shooting stick, a device used to rest the barrel of the gun on to steady the rifle when you have nothing else to use. I could not use it because the down slope I was sitting on was too steep, making the shooting stick too low. Instead, I jumped up, ran down about ten more feet, sat on my rear and wrapped the gun strap around my left elbow and put both elbows between my knees, my favorite shooting position.

"Kaa-boom!"

I hit him and he stumbled then he got up and ran away. He did not run too far and I was on him immediately and shot again, I did not want him to get away this time. Then he disappeared.

Partner did not see where he fell or if he fell but I did. I heard the bullet hit and the buck was hurt bad although, he walked to the other side of a Palo Verde tree then he disappeared.

It took some time to get to the place where the buck was hit the first time. I tracked him to the second place I shot and worked maybe, 25 yards further. When we could not find him we started making spiraling circles around the last known place of the deer. My heart was failing. I began to wonder, perhaps I did miss him.

Finally, after quite sometime I almost stumbled over the deer lying in the shade on the ground. He was so perfectly camouflaged. He had truly walked only two steps from the last shot and fell. We were looking too far out thinking he could have moved some distance. We found that both shots were fatal shots and we were both surprised that it took two shots to down him.

It was a nice deer, a three by three, nice beams that curled perfectly to the front. I was happy my time had arrived and the pack-out was not as difficult as it had been the day before.

When everyone returned to camp, it was told that two of the other hunters were perched on top of the mountain above us, two miles away. They had watched the whole event through spotting scopes and they said they had the best show watching me run around, take two shots and loosing the deer for a while. They assured me that they were telling me where to go and giving all kinds of directions as if I could hear them. Their direction was as effective as talking to a television screen. Even so, they felt like they had been there and had participated in my success. Their stories would be a little different than mine because their perspective was blurry and slanted with their own jokes.

I want more bucks!

I am fairly sure that I will get the satisfaction and feel very successful when I find the perfect deer and take the perfect first-shot.

A little Arizona mule deer

Ludicrous

I was in Unit 9 hunting for a trophy elk. It rained so hard the ground sunk under my feet twelve inches. Then it snowed twelve inches. Then the fog rolled in and sucked all the air out of the land and then we got stuck and stranded.

I was not having fun.

I suppose when surroundings get this way, the buddy system is a necessity if not for help, companionship. A buddy can help you keep your sense of humor and strengthen you enough to do what needs to be done as things worsen through the hours.

We were living in a barrowed tent trailer. These types of rigs are not made for high-country bad, snowy, foggy, wet weather although, we thought, we are tough, it is probably better than a tent and it was offered so we took it.

The inside was a hideous teal-greenish color painted ceiling, sides, and floor and that made me feel even worse. It was tight quarters and cold inside all the time because the sides are made of canvas. They are equipped with pull-out beds that protrude over the outer edges of the trailer from both ends and when extended, there is nothing around or under the thin bed platform except for canvas.

We tried to hunt, and could only maneuver right at sunrise because the ground was frozen solid at that time. The freeze only lasted two hours. We had to time our short hunt so we could rush back to the tent trailer. If we did not make it in time, we sunk! I mean we just sunk—twelve inches deep in the muck making it impossible to walk or maneuver using any mode of transportation.

One time out, we found and watched a mom, dad and three little puppy fox come out of their den and romp around. That was special.

Once we tried to take the quad into a high-ground area where we planned to walk around for a time but it sunk. We had to leave it, walking back to the tent trailer where we waited for the ground to freeze again so that we could retrieve it.

The day before, we did not make it back within the allotted two hours and had managed to bury the truck in a vehicle made river with a mud bottom. It took us three hours to finally get out of that mess. I feel sure that the truck would still be there and that we would not have made it out if it had not been for those other crazy hunters trying to maneuver around our stuck truck.

They said that they felt so sorry for us, that they would use their tow chain to try to pull us out even though it was very probable that they would be stuck over night with us. We laughed sort of, nothing was too funny by this time, and asked about possible provisions should that occur. They did not have provisions and we did not either. There would be no rewards for the hard work ahead.

They did get stuck but got out and they did manage to free us after a lot of thinking, physical work and vehicle jerking and tugging. That was a sticky day. Then we went back to the tent trailer to suffer through another night.

We played Gin Rummy until we could not see the spots on the cards. We ran out of food and camp medicine by day four. The little generator we used to keep the little furnace going had broken after two nights. We used all the propane cooking and keeping the stove top burners going for warmth and we ran out of water. That is when we finally decided that we just could not stand it another moment. At that point we did not even care if the weather cleared. We decided to take a nap, wake up at midnight and drive like a banshee runs hopefully, making it out before the next thaw.

To prepare for the run, we packed everything, closed everything up, hitched the trailer and stayed in the truck until it was time. I sat with my rifle next to me just in case some crazy bull elk happened to walk by while I waited. That did not happen.

At midnight we took off, bouncing and sliding around but we were not sinking. We had decided to take the long way around because there was a little creek bottom filled with rocks that we planned to drive through while frozen for traction.

We talked about the fact there was some risk involved because going the long way, would take us farther out and away from possible help. If we got stuck it would be very unlikely that anyone could get to us before spring. We would have to think up something else and save ourselves if that happens.

The ground was frozen and we only sank a little; I learned that is when you hit the accelerator and spin out as fast as you can. Luckily, the whole plan worked out all right.

It was 6:00 a.m. when our truck tires hit blacktop. It had taken us six hours to drive forty miles. I still had my sense of humor but I believe the whole experience was the most ludicrous hunting trip that I have ever attempted. I swore I was giving up hunting, never wanted to do it again, and I truly hate that teal-green color to this day.

The whole pursuit was not a hunt, it was about surviving. It was learning how to get along with others even when you do not feel like it—I guess it was about working together until you can get it done or get out in this case.

Bull elk caught unaware in northern Arizona

Collared Peccary

"Where did he go? Cut him off around that tree. Don't let him den up in that hole or get in the drain pipe. Watch out! I see him! He's over there. Get 'em, Get 'em! I got him! He's up, shoot again!"

These are the sounds I am hearing as the five of us are running around on the highway median at mile post 208 on Interstate Highway 17 chasing wild pigs. What a hoot! This is the most fun I have had in a very long time. The event is comical, silly and so much fun.

Arrows were being flung all over the place. Four archers were trying their best to stick the javelina running around us, the bushes, through and up the ravine, then over a little hill. Two of the pigs were running about with arrows stuck into their side and the arrows were bouncing around as if it did not faze them. A vehicle stopped on the highway to see what the fuss was all about. I could see them pointing at us and heard them laughing hysterically as all of us dashed up the hill and down the other side chasing those pigs with bows drawn, quivers swinging from side straps, screaming directions or commands all the while. Come to think of it, the noise we were making obviously terrified and confused the pigs into acting more than unusual. That alone was something to watch.

The pigs kicked up little tuffs of dust when they abruptly turned to face off the predator-hunter. Then in a state of confusion they turned then run up another little hill. It could have appeared to another that we were chasing little dust clouds because the javelina constantly eluded us by diving into a bush becoming virtually invisible even while standing five feet away.

Someone pulled out their pistol which was legal then, and shot one but the little thing got up and disappeared. I wonder if he just simply missed the animal; too close or the hunter was shaking too much from laughing.

These animals are incredibly camouflaged and they sometimes freeze when scared and you truly can not see them unless they move or snort or snap and chomp their teeth. A javelina is a very tough little thing. They can take a real beating and live. They chomp their teeth when they get mad too so, a hunter must be aware and always ready to run away.

The herd of wild pigs eventually ran through a culvert that ran under the northbound highway and to the other side, unfortunately the other side was also another hunt unit so we could not chase them there.

When it was all finished, we had two nice bores to take home.

Javelina, as the Mexicans call them are mean vicious little rodents. They are from the rodent animal family and I do not know why we call them wild pigs because of that. Their official name is collared peccary. They root for food and bugs like a pig, they are 30-130 pounds, they are virtually blind only seeing movement, shadows and perhaps color change although, they have extremely sharp hearing. They are noted for aggressiveness and will chase you and bite you, defensively because they are blind.

They have really ugly hair, not furry hair but sticker course black and grey hair. They stink. I mean really stink and you can smell them from a long distance. They kind of contaminate the area with their smell. A hunter usually smells them long before spying them. They do not even taste good unless you pit barbeque them, slowly and for a very long time. When cooked that way, they do taste much like pork.

These little varmints run around in herds from three to thirty. They are most plentiful in cactus, desert areas although, they live in snow country as well.

One time, I was accompanying partner on an archery javelina hunt in the Bull Pin area close to Camp Verde. He flung five arrows at the little thing and stuck him two times. From the chase and the arrow wounds the pig laid down under a juniper tree to rest. Partner had shot all of his arrows, two still sticking out of the pig's side and he told me to stand there and watch the pig while he looked for some of his shot arrows. He could not use a pistol then because it was illegal.

"Why don't you try to video the javelina while I go look for the arrows?"

"I already got some great shots but I will. How close do you think I can get?"

"Close. Just watch him because he may move and if he does, we will never find him again."

I approached the javelina and got within ten feet of it. I did not want to scare him more than he already was and used the zoom lens to look at his vampire fangs, his eyes, his ears, and his hoofs, and his haunch hair because it sticks up and bushes out like thorns on the top of a barrel cactus. The arrows stuck in him were not deep and he did not seem to be in much discomfort, just hot and tired. About then, the little varmint jumped to his feet, standing on all four at once and stood there staring at me. Then he chomped his teeth and stomped his hoof and huffed. Then that little mean sucker charged at me.

"Holy Moly, he's up! He's chasing me! Oh, he just bit my heel! Shoot him Ricky, shoot him! Hurry up! Shoot him, shoot him!"

I am running for my life. I had no idea that pigs can run so fast, especially a wounded one! I was jumping cactus, screaming and running as fast as I can but that little thing is right on me snapping his teeth together over and over. He sounds like a demon. In fact, I am positive that is exactly what he is. He is biting my ankle and heel and I trip and stumble to keep from falling down because if I did, that thing would probably kill me. He has hold of the back of my foot. I rip it out of his vice grip teeth and try to get away. I have already run more than 50 yards and that pig will not stop!

Where in the world is that hunter with those arrows? This pig must die!

Then, I figure it will sure be funny to take a movie with this video camera that is still strapped to my wrist. Still running, I twist around to try to point the camera down and at it. I push the go button and I am sure that I got the pig filmed while it is right on my heels. I hope that I have him in the lens because there is no way that I can see through it and run like a wild hysterical screaming child across the mountain side at the same time.

Ouch! Ouch! He gets me again.

Finally, archer is running sort of parallel to me. I can see he has an arrow, only one. He knocks the arrow and draws.

"Swish," I hear the sound of the arrow and see it sail over the pig's back.

Good grief! How long will this take?

Archer runs after the arrow he just shot. Gets it, nocks it, and takes aim again. This time, the arrow hits hard and in the right place and that pig drops hard to the ground. I was leery because the pig just might be tired or faking it. By now I am convinced that one can not kill a javelina even though it deserves to die after what he did to me. I am not in any hurry to poke him to check and watch the archer closely as he does.

"What a relief, you finally got the little sucker! He is dead! What took you so long? Wait until you see this film. Oh my, look what it did to my leather boot, it is ripped and my poor ankle hurts but my ankle is not torn to bits like it feels it should be. I am so happy that thing is dead!" That is all I could say before I was overtaken with loud laughter. The whole thing seemed quite funny afterwards.

Once, we caught our breath again, I checked the camera hoping to relive what just happened to me. The camera was on pause, all along. I had pushed the wrong stupid button on the video camera. There were no pictures. That caused my biggest disappointment of that day because if I had been successful at filming the pig chasing me, at that range, with me screaming all the while, I may have won the prize for funniest home video and people would believe me when I tell them I was chased by a wild pig and barely lived through it.

Another time, deer hunting we took a little break and sat on a bluff edge to glass the other side of the cut. A great big bore snuck up behind partner, sniffed him with his nose and grunted. That pig came out of no where and it scared partner so bad that he could not breathe for five minutes as his reaction was to jump and run away and he fell down the first little ridge and hurt himself, scratches and a sprained ankle, just trying to get away. I feel sorry but I laughed so hard that the tears squirted out of my eyes.

Why do we laugh at someone else's fear and accidents? I do not know but we do.

Another season, five were hunting the javelina and another hunter and I crossed the dry creek bed to try to spot a herd that had meander all around us for over an hour. We could not get on to them so we thought it would be a good idea to watch from the other side then we would signal the hunter on the pig's side giving location and direction.

We spotted them from the other side, the pigs were truly only five feet from the archer and he could not see them. We used signals and radios to communicate, and it was funny and frustrating to watch how the animals eluded the archer by running around the archer, around bushes, hiding in rocks, and then scampering away to their secret places. Who is the blind one, archer or pig?

Humans are so inept compared to a wild pig and I think all other animals. I do not think there is such a thing as fair chase. The animals always have the advantage. They just accidentally make a mistake occasionally and get caught. Then we call them what they truly are, kamikazes.

I recall a time when an archer was hunting in the Tucson foothills and he came across a herd of javelina but could not get close enough to shoot one; he had chased them all around for hours before he did. He made an excellent shot; it looked like a heart-shot, half the arrow shaft sticking out one side and the arrow tip out the opposite side. Do you think that pig would fall down dead? No. It ran down hill, into a patch of prickly pear cactus, no bushes, no holes, no hiding place to be found although, the pig was certainly looking for his secret place.

The pig was running and darting around so quickly that the archer could not take a second bow and arrow shot, if he even had an arrow. So, being a seasoned hunter, he dropped his bow and pulled his Bowey knife from his belt, growled like a wolf, flexed his muscles, stuck the knife blade between his front teeth and ran after the wounded pig. It was a big bore and he could not let that one go.

Eventually, after quite a show of him running all over the side of the hill in hot pursuit, right on the pig's back hooves, too close that the pig being scared almost to death did not have a second to turn on him, to reverse the chase, he was able to literally jump on the back of that pig and he stabbed it to death while riding it.

Another story, this man was walking the desert with his dog and a javelina popped out angry because it did not like the dog. The pig started chasing the dog and grabbed the dog's hind leg. The man was so mad that he grabbed the pig by the scruff of the neck and jerked with all his might until the pig let go of the dog's leg. The dog yipped away with a very serious wound. Then the pig being held in a most precarious way turned his head and chomped down on the man's forearm and would not let go.

The man pulled that pig attached to his arm to the truck parked some yards away, and thank goodness the passenger window was down so that he could reach in and grab his .45 pistol. The man had to shoot the pig to get it to release his poor ripped, bleeding arm.

These little rodents deserve to be killed or totally left alone, but they are funny and they are a hoot to watch and hunt. They are most entertaining and there is no question in my mind that they have the advantage over any hunter, they get away more than not, and they do some important things, like kill rattle snakes and that is the only important thing I can think of. Otherwise, they do have a demon nature, they destroy every type of vegetation they root and browse through, they stink to high heaven, they are aggressive and very mean and they bite!

Little Shiner

"Jig fishing, using a little live shiner guarantees a catch. When no other bait or lure works the little flashy minnow sized shiner fish at the end of a hook will do the job."

He was explaining this while he rigged his pole for a cast into water known to boast ten-pound bass. There was a size slot limit, only the very big ones were keepers. The rule was that the fish had to weigh over five pounds, any smaller had to be thrown back.

Then he made his cast, a nice one, almost to other side. He started reeling in slowly jerking the pole tip lightly every other turn of the reel.

Bam! Something struck the bait.

Jerking upward with the pole to set the hook was a natural reaction. Two seconds later, the fish jumped at least a foot into the air, a nice fat one. More line wound in and the rhythm of the catch underway.

Splash! The fish jumps again and before it splashed back into the water a great big bird grabbed it in a swooping motion with a dead ahead flight pattern set to collide and crash into the fisherman. Before fisherman could decipher what was happening, the bird was flopping wildly in front of his face slapping him around with its wings at the same time trying to turn and gain altitude.

"Holy Moly! What was that?" he screamed as he turned to the side, tugging on his pole, straightening out his line and making an awkward stumbling attempt to gain some balance.

Swoosh! The bird turned to fly the other way. It looked like it was a flying drunkard, dizzy and all over the place, up and down and sideways.

The bird finally regained some flying skill as it balanced out and flew out over the water, the other way. As it was skimming the water top, I saw its head jerk and then its legs flipped over its belly like he was doing a backwards somersault. Then I realized that the fishing line had become taught and when it did, the bird was jerked to an immediate halt, like it ran into an invisible wall or like a ball on the end of a rubber band stringed paddle.

I had never seen a live bird float on its back with both wings flopped out to its sides. I did not know they could do that.

That bird once righted, did some adjusting and tucking of its wings and just sat there still as a grounded bush poking out of the water for a second then he shook his head back and forth and tried to throw-up the fish in its throat but he could not because the fishing line had somehow got twisted and wrapped around its pelican beak, probably during the somersault trick.

That was an amazing site. A choking crazy pelican all wrapped up with a great big bass stuck in its throat and a fisherman trying to reel the bird in. The pole was jerking and bending to an extreme downward curve due to the resisting bird and its weight.

The pole should have snapped but it did not. I decided that the fisherman must be using an Ugly Stick the one that the lady on TV tries to destroy as she jams the rod into a trash compactor while yelling that her husband can not go fishing that day.

The fisherman, beside himself did not want to hurt the bird. He knew that if he cut the line, the beak would still be wrapped all up and the bird would die because it would not be able to ever eat again. The fish in his throat would be its last.

That pelican sat there on the water as the fisherman tugged lightly on the fishing line until the bird was floating with its beak facing the fisherman. At that point the fisherman lifted his pole tip and made big circular motions that enabled somehow, the unwrapping of the fishing line from the birds' beak. Once loosed, the bird shook its head violently and gagged repeatedly stretching its neck then tucking it against its breast. It had swallowed the fish and it was a big one, too big to go down or come up easily. I could see the giant lump in the birds' neck. The fisherman kept the fishing line tight so that it would not get tangled around the bird again. It was hilarious to see the fishing line shimmer out of the birds' beak and it getting towed and tugged around like it was a remote control water toy.

The bird flopped, splashed, choked and finally the big fish popped out and back into the water. The bird must have nearly killed itself dislodging the fish because it did not fly away it just sat there and glared at the fisherman. I mean that bird looked mad, angry as if it were planning some recoiling attack. I actually thought about running into the woods to get away.

Fisherman started reeling in the rest of his line. When revealed, a big bass was still hooked. When the fisherman took the fish off the hook, that little wiggly shiner was still alive and flipping around.

"What a shame, after getting slapped around by a crazy pelican and all of that other stuff happened, I have to throw this fish back. It is too small," fisherman sadly declared.

Fisherman checked the line and made a little adjustment to the little shiner on the hook and made another cast. As he slowly reeled in the line he looked over with a grin as wide as an ocean horizon.

"See? I told you so. A little live shiner guarantees that you will catch something!"

Tangled Up

"Easy little deer, it will be okay. I need to get you untangled and out of this fence," he said softly as he slowly approached the twisted barbwire fence that had wrapped around the fawn's hind leg at the ankle. The barbs were tight and gouged into the deer. It was tearing its hide and the leg was bleeding slightly but the man could tell the injury would not cripple the deer if he could free it soon.

The young man was tall and lean and he was pretty sure that he could bend over the top wire of the fence. There may be slight tension across his stomach, just under his chest. The fence may protect him from the frightened, struggling, kicking deer because he would be leaning over it and on the other side of the fence. Then he would grab hold of the deer leg to try to slack the wire enough to pull the leg out and free the young animal, just a small humanitarian thing to do.

He had been driving his route, making a routine delivery when he witnessed the little deer attempt to jump the fence and when that failed the animal stuck its head through the lowest space in between two strands of barbed wire to step through to the other side and when the wire scrapped the front of its leg, the deer freaked out and kicked and fell somehow causing the first wire to twist with the second wire that snared the leg. The deer was in a panic state and the approach of a human made it react frantically, turning, struggling and kicking. It flashed frightful eyes that looked big and wide as a tea cup.

The man, after placing his upper body over the wire reached down to grab the leg. Before he knew what happened, he realized that he had been whipped and thrown over the top wire, his legs sticking straight out, dangling down sort of bouncing in the air, hands flat on the ground on the opposite side. He guessed the deer had knocked a post loose somewhere close by while it was kicking and struggling making the fence give and tip, his own weight toppling him over. Then the fence must have bounced back into the standing position snagging him in a recoiling action.

The deer under him was kicking the living daylights out of his belly and chest. He felt his stomach was being poked and scratched by the barbs. Then the little stinker kicked him just under his eye, while the other sharp hoof jabbed into his gut and chest with incredible strength.

The lower eye cheek area is a very sensitive place and being sliced open by the hoof it began to bleed profusely and blood ran right into his eye. Now he could not see very well because blood blurs the vision. He noticed that his own blood did not sting when it got into his eye.

His shirt was caught on a couple of barbs to the point he could not push himself off the top wire. When he tried to spring himself up by pushing off with his hands from the other side, he just bounced. His feet could not catch the ground because they never reached it.

His next brilliant move was to try to flip the feet and legs over the fence backwards. When he tried that, he found himself in a handstand position and he was stuck firmly to the barbed fence, not only his shirt firmly snagged but the barbs had grabbed the fly of his pants, where the fabric is reinforce and too strong to just tear. His whole body was parallel to the fence. He was up-side-down pole-like hanging there getting stuck in more places, with a bad headache developing, feeling dizzy and his eye hurt. He figured that the blood dripping up his chest would stop soon. It sort of tickled. He wished that he did not have to take the blood thinner prescribed to him because this whole situation could get worse. He could hear his mom warn, "If you bleed stop it because it could leak out too fast."

He opened his eyes and found his face was next to the deer's head. His hands straddled the deer's body. That deer was not a happy animal.

During the man flipping act, the deer turned, twisting its leg tighter in the wire and it was scrapping the ground with its front hooves, making the strangest yelping, grunting noise in a desperate attempt to escape being squashed by the crazy upside down human who was heavily breathing on it.

"Hey, be quiet, just calm it down!"

His words just scared the deer more. He thought he should pet the animal but did not want to receive another kick. A few seconds past then viewing the situation in his closer position, he noticed that the deer's leg seemed to have moved to the little space in between two barbs. The man could hold himself somewhat steady with one arm so he reached to loosen the barbwire from the deer's leg with the other. He struggled to get his hand in between the two wire strands just far enough to make a gap and the deer wriggled its leg and hoof out of the entanglement.

"Look what you made me do! At least you are freed. I think I'm into it worse than you were," he said aloud hanging there up-side-down looking at the deer that had managed to move a few yards away before it stopped and stared back at the man.

"No way, I don't need your help. Go away you mean thing! I was trying to do you favor, the right thing, and look what happened because of that!"

That deer stayed there along time before it finally dashed off to find its mother.

The man hung, resting a little as he tried to think. There was not much of a chance that someone would drive by and see him and even if there was, he sure did not want to be found while in this predicament. If he had a pocket knife he would cut himself free although he could see that it had dropped out of his pocket and it was lying on the other side of the fence out of reach.

Right about then he felt his pants tear. He felt his pant waist loosen and he could feel the zipper slowly sliding down. He started dropping out of his pants. He had boots on his feet and he knew the pant leg would not slip over the boots. He struggled using his hands and arms and sort of pulled himself up sideways using the strands of barbwire ladder-like to pull and push up to reach his boot lace. He was finally successful at untying one boot and somehow got it off.

"Bop," the heavy boot dropped right onto his head then flopped to the ground.

"Ouch!"

It was a hard thing to do. He was not that limber but he managed to slip the rest of the bootless foot out of his pants. He eventually managed to twist and turn and reach and pull and tear until his other pant leg loosed from the barbed grip. It hurt. The barbs scraped and dug deep into the skin.

Once he found himself righted and on his feet again, he was standing there pant less. He was bleeding from the pokes like he had been darted fifty-five times. His pants and shirt were shredded, lots of tiny holes and little rips in them. The shirt front looked almost like a cat had clawed and scraped him down and upwards. The pant waistband was hanging by a thread so he could not fasten them once pulled up and his hips were too thin and they would not stay up. He found a piece of non-barbed fence wire and wired his pants to his shirt tail using the holes already made.

He struggled and stumbled back to his truck. Climbed in and drove down the road to his delivery destination, the prison. Frankly, he could not do anything about how he looked but he figured it could not be too bad, a little dirty maybe, he reasoned as he drove up to the first check point.

He gave the wave and a nod to the entrance guard as usual but the guard called him to stop. The guard asked him about the black eye and cut under it.

He told him a deer kicked him but that he was alright now. As he drove up to the receiving door he wondered if the first guard had heard what he said because he did not really responded, he just waved him through.

Then he got out of the truck with papers in hand and entered the building to go through the second routine check point. The guard took one look at him and pressed the alarm that triggered a full prison lock down, and then he immediately called for paramedics and an ambulance as alarms blared.

"It was just a deer."

"What?"

"I'm beat up and I have blood all over me because the deer kicked me and I got stuck in a barbed wire fence."

"Where are you stabbed? Where's the guy that did this? What the hell happened to you?" the guard repeatedly asked.

"I was just trying to do the right thing and get the little deer out of the fence."

"God bless, man, sit down here, rest, the ambulance is on its way. Tell me what happened and who did this to you!" All the while men were running around, pulling on bullet protection vests, yelling orders, grabbing defense and assault gear from lockers and other vaulted areas.

"I've told you three times. Bambi did it! You know the little deer in the woods? I got attacked by a mean little deer! Look you can see the hoof imprint where he kicked me. It is right here," he declared, as he lifted his shredded shirt and pointed to the black and bluish, perfectly formed hoof mark on his chest.

It took three different prison personnel to get one that actually listened to the whole story then they could not believe it, and ask him to tell it again. The paramedics were the ones who convinced the prison personnel that he had not been stabbed by an inmate. The puncture holes were not deep or big enough.

Everyone seemed to be taking their time and they had it because once a shut-down happens at a high security prison it can not be called off. They have to do all kinds of things before they can unlock any area, especially an exit.

It was three hours later when the man walked out of the secured fortress and to his truck. As he drove down the highway he concentrated not to look to the side into the woods. He swore he would never try to save a wild animal again. He could not afford to because if something can go wrong, it would surly be happening to him. He tugged up at his loose pants and touched his sore eye bone area that had swelled up nicely in spite of the care he had gotten at the prison.

"I was just trying to do a humanitarian thing, the right thing. I won't do that again . . ." he thought in a transitive, deep and serious, dreamy way.

The prison guards call him Bambi when he arrives for a delivery. It is not a good name, one he wished he had not earned but how he earned it does make him chuckle privately and with the passage of time, he is sort of getting used to it, just sort of.

Goose Shoots

We like to go to the Verde River to do duck and geese hunting probably because it is the only river close enough to take a day hunt and because there are some little pond areas that you can throw some decoys out and hide on the shore to wait and wait and watch and watch. The set-up can be pretty boring actually.

"Way up there, against the cliff, sitting, there are some Canada geese!"

"I'll sneak up there and try to get them to fly. You stay here and shoot when they fly over. They always fly down river, you might get a shot!"

"I need to cross the river because they are going to fly over that ridge, sure as can be," I replied.

I had some time because the sneak would take at least thirty minutes but all the while, I must stay out of sight. Geese have incredible sight. If they see me they will most likely flare and go up river before he has a chance to take a shot, when they fly off the water and get out of range. Then, having experience in these matters, the geese will turn back, fly over a high ridge and land one to two miles down river. One can chase these birds all day long and never get a shot.

The river is running deep here. I need to go around the bend and cross there. It was too far of a hike to carry waders. I decide to keep my boots and socks on my feet to cross. I do roll up my pants as high as I can. It is January and the water is so cold. My boots are old and I do not care if they get ruined by a soaking and they will dry out sooner or later and it is too slippery and my feet too tender to go barefoot, I reason.

I slip on the slimy river rocks anyway, and catch myself from falling all the way in, drenching my coat sleeve up to my arm pit. Only that much wet, I am shivering and my feet are so cold they are stiff. No choice but to brave up and keep going.

I get to the other side and I must take my boots and socks off to wring them out. Sitting there to do that, I am anxiously watching the sky and my dog sits right next to me on my left side, just like she is trained to do because I shoot right-handed.

"Good grief, here they come!" I tell her.

Swooshing wings and the familiar, honk-honk-honk, can not be mistaken for anything else.

Right over me and to the left, only two seconds to get it together, find the lead bird, pull through it at least a bird's length, squeeze the trigger and keep the swing of the gun in motion or I will shoot behind or under the bird.

Ka-boom!

The goose flares. I can tell it is hit because feathers are wafting downward.

Ka-boom!

Wings fold as it drops from the sky with the second shot into the river. Oh no, I wanted him to fall on the ground.

Dog jumps and hits the water hard swimming with all her might. Goose in sight and she is closing the distance in between her and the goose fast. But, there it goes down river and my bird dog can not swim fast enough in the current.

As my faithful dog jumped in the river, I jump to my feet, grab my gun and start running down the bank as fast as I can. About twelve feet into my dash I painfully realize that I do not have anything on my poor old feet. Ouch, Ouch, Ouchy! I am yelling while jumping over reeds and rocks and there are lots of stickers.

I run into the bluff and can go no farther after my jaunting for at least 500 yards along the river bank. There is no way around it. There is no use to even jump into the river and swim around it. Darn! I can see my goose floating away and my dog still swimming after it tenaciously. I can see that there is too much distance between the dog and the goose.

That is a shame. That was my very first Canada goose and I lost it. Sometimes that happens. The only consolation is that it will provide food for another animal or bird along the way. We just could not retrieve my prize that day. My thoughts were sad and regretful and I hugged my dog for all her efforts when she finally returned. She knew it was lost too.

By then my partner had come within yelling distance. He saw me make the shot and commented that it was a beautiful shot, hard to do in the second of opportunity.

"Were you sitting on the bank when you shot? Why did you do that?"

Then he looked at my feet and had to say, "Only you would run down a riverbank barefoot because only you would take your boots off right before the action. And only you could have made the shot while you were doing all that stuff you were not suppose to be doing!"

"I had to. My socks and boots were wet and gushy."

I had another opportunity to get a goose, another year and day in January sitting on a bluff at Mormon Lake. That day it was so cold that the steam of my own breath could not find rise once released from my mouth. Everything in the air just hung in a fog in an iced atmosphere.

It was another miserable day and I have no idea why I even try to participate when I know that I will suffer much.

Two hours had past of which I was cuddled up against a rock in an attempt to stay out of the icy breeze. Every now and then I would glance up to the look-out point about two miles away, to gaze at the big motor home sitting there full of my family who were drinking coffee and cocoa while the bacon sizzled in the fry pan. The windows were all foggy but I could see them and I could smell the bacon too.

Finally, geese decide to fly off the lake and they were coming straight into me, honking while forming their V flight pattern; such a beautiful sight and sound. As they came into range, I took my aim and when I pulled at the trigger my finger did not bend. It was frozen. Actually, my finger was not frozen but the heavy glove on it was as if I had a splint wrapped around it. Because of that, the finger of the glove could not fit into the trigger guard to pull the trigger.

Two other shooters got their geese because that had not happened to them.

The only thing good about that adventure was the relief I felt when I finally reached the refuge sitting at the look-out and I got to eat that bacon and drink that coffee.

There was one more opportunity for me to get a goose: we were walking in a canyon that had a little river running through it, during a javelina archery hunt. The place is called Dry Beaver Creek. This stream is usually dry but it was running because of heavy snow run-off and a healthy rainy season that year.

I was not archery hunting but I was carrying a shot gun in hopes of catching a duck resting on this stream on its way to the Verde River and I could also shoot a quail.

"Look, goose tracks in the sand on this bank and they are fresh tracks."

"It could be molting, although it is a little early for that. Maybe it is just resting up from its long flight from Canada."

"Hurry, change the shells in your shotgun, you need a heavier number 4 shot."

We walked another few feet and we both jumped back when a big Canada goose waddled out of a bush in front of us only five feet from our boots. When it started to run, we ran after it and the archer tried to stab it with the arrow he was carrying in his hand. That did not work because the goose dodged the arrow as it hissed madly at us.

We found ourselves running around in circles chasing that goose more. I was as ready as I could be to shoot but I could not shoot the goose running around. Good grief, if I shot him with the number 4 shell at that close range it will blow the bird into bits. I would be tarred and feathered if I shot at that range. It needed to fly.

The archer was right in front of me and he knocked the arrow and drew back his bow to shoot. That is when I pushed him!

"Stop it! That is my goose!"

Then the archer turned on me and tried to pull the shot gun out of my hands!

While we are fighting over the gun, the goose is still running around in front of us. By the time we settled our differences I still held the gun and I shouldered it ready to shoot as we commenced to chasing the goose. Now I was in the front position, archer chasing after me and me hot on the goose's tail pointing my gun barrel at it all the while.

Finally, that goose took flight and I shot.

I shot behind the thing and it was out of range before I could pull again. Immediately after the shot, a pintail drake duck jumped off the water right in line of my gun sight and I shot him. The duck fell to the water and I jumped in the stream, ran over and grabbed him quick.

"Ha-ha," I laughed.

"I've got no goose in my bag, but a pretty little prize of a duck instead."

We had a little talk about who gets to do what and that he better not ever try to grab my gun away even if he feels too excited or that I may be too slow at taking aim. I told him that I would shoot him if he ever tried to do that again.

Right of Passage

We called him CM because even when he was younger he could see'em—everything that moved in the forests, and he called out the names of animals and critters as easily as letters in the alphabet.

"That's a deer-buck. That's a squirrel. That's an elk. That's a loper," his word for antelope. "That's a turkey. That's a horned toad. There's another jackrabbit."

He had reached ten years of age and had just completed hunter safety, first in his class, the night before he shot his first gobbler turkey. A couple of months later we took him on his first elk hunt. He had drawn to hunt in unit 5B. I planned to go along because I had a part in CM's learning about hunting and besides, I had a permit to hunt bull elk.

The area is diverse including canyons, flat red-sand desert, ridges that top-out in ponderosa pine and in between is the elk's favorite type of browsing habitat that hosts cedar trees for cover and various grasses and plenty of water.

We managed to gain permission to use a cattleman's old rickety cabin to stay in while hunting; they call it Walldrop Place. I do not know why they called it that. The place could have been named after a cowboy or because the ridge broke straight off of Anderson Mesa. The closest ridge did look like the wall had simply broke away and dropped off thus, some cowboy's description of the place where the wall dropped.

It is an original Babbitt Ranch cowboy cabin built in the early 1900s. Babbitt Ranch was founded by four brothers and the ranch covers many acres in northern Arizona. The Babbitt brothers worked together to develop a huge cattle ranch business and they are credited for economic development in northern Arizona.

This little cabin is one of many scattered throughout the land that the ranchers built and used while they tended cattle. Walldrop Place was usually occupied year-round during the ranching eras because it sits lower in elevation, it is in the middle of summer and winter pasture, and it was just simply habitable. Babbitt Ranch is still a working ranch although Walldrop Place has not been lived in by cowboys for several years but they visit it. Cowboys drive trucks now, and they ride ATVs instead of their horses most of the time and they do not have to stay in the wilderness for months at a time any longer.

The cabin had an old wood burning cook stove, lots of mice running around, a decaying outhouse and a barn that was standing even though leaning to one side, about twenty feet from the only doorway into the cabin. The old buildings were a faded dirty green color, the floors were chancy in places, and the wind blew in between the one-by-six inch slats that created walls. The cabin roof was tin and there was an old well with no water in it just outside to the right of the entrance door to the cabin.

As you entered the cabin there was a four-foot-by-four-foot area where the wood burning cook stove sat and around it were ancient counter tops made of scrap one-by-twelve inch pine that made the work area for the kitchen. A long time ago, someone whitewashed the counters and walls. On one side of the stove the counter top was hinged and under it, there was a wood box. Next to that, one of the old wall slats was sawed out in between the wall studs and then hinges were added to the cut out part making a skinny little door. Inside were skinny little shelves and there was a box of wood matches sitting on one shelf and a couple of old tea bags. The cooking place was a very efficient use of a small area.

Directly across from the entrance was a small doorway that opened into a larger room where we could lay six or more bedrolls and stash our gear. It smelled old but it was not too bad. I used an old piece of newspaper tin-type that I found blowing around outside to place over a drafty hole in the floor, close to the far side of the big room. I nailed that down with a rock using old crooked rusty nails I found laying around the barn.

The larger room was furnished with a tiny little metal four-legged, gold speckled white Formica topped table with four skinny chairs sitting around it. I think the table and chairs were 1920s vintage and it looked like it came out of a tiny camp trailer. A table leaf was inserted that was only four inches wide. Wonder why they bothered with that?

On one wall an old faded black and white picture of a horse was held up with a rusty thumbtack and that was the only decoration. It was a very rustic environment, very livable. We planned to stay a week and moved in immediately.

It was Thanksgiving time and CM's family planned to come out on that day and cook a whole stuffed turkey in the old cook stove. We planned to eat a feast of all the traditional Thanksgiving foods with everyone who could get there to join us.

CM drew the any elk permit and the odds of him getting one were high because it did not matter if he got a calf, cow or bull, of course a bull would be the best of all outcomes. We had three tags to fill, CM's, mine and grandfather's. Gramps was hopeful to shoot a cow elk for the meat. We talked about that while we got settled into the place then we all went outside to glass the side of the ridge where at the top, the wall had dropped. The land sharply inclined directly behind the cabin, the ridge was a likely place to see elk that time of day.

I noticed that the sun was on its setting track, just to the right side of us. The ridge shadowed the cabin by four o'clock. There are a lot of country choices around us and the visual distance in all directions, very good. These things add up to nearly perfect hunting conditions. After a look around, we went back inside to study the area map and make opening morning plans.

Day one we would split up, one group to go up the ridge to the southeast, a couple would go north and the other west then northwest. We wanted to personally see what was in the area and find where a concentration of elk might be. CM, his dad and I decided to explore west which also included Elliott Canyon and Anderson Mesa ridge.

We hunted all day from sun-up to sun-down and did not find one elk. An unexpected storm was moving in and it was cold when we got back to the cabin. We had covered at least twelve square miles. There was fresh track around all the water holes, and we found scrapes on the barbed fences where elk hair had been pulled or scrape off when they jumped over it. The elk were there. We just could not see or find them that day.

Grandma had arrived with CM's little seven-year-old sister.

Sister explained, "Grandma and she, would play cards, do puzzles, knit, tell stories, color in coloring books, cook, take walks and discuss important things while the hunters were out all day."

Sitting around eating dinner that evening, everyone else reported what they found during the day. CM's grandfather thought he saw the rear end of an elk disappearing into the cedars. Grandfather had an any-elk permit also, but the shot could not be taken.

"The elk was on the sly, sneaking away from its mighty predator," he explained to CM, with aiming animation, big eyes, and exaggerated Elmer Fudd wrabbitt-sneaking giant steps.

More stories were told that night when the lanterns were turned off as we all lay around in our bedrolls attempting to fall asleep. CM started telling dirty jokes showing amazing memorization skills and he surprised us with his ten-year-old perception because he obviously did not know the meaning of the terms and things he was talking about. As he made his point about what he did not know, I laughed so hard that I cried.

The next morning, Grandma's pajamas were mysteriously turned wrong side out and the shirt tag was sticking up in her neck line. CM could not imagine how that could have happened and he worried about that as he ate a sweet roll for breakfast.

"I sure hope my cloths don't do that to me while I sleep."

The next morning, he declared that he did not sleep well because he had to hold his shirt on all night.

It was day two of the hunt. Grandfather went back to the spot where he got a glimpse of an elk. We took off in the same direction as before. About noon it began to snow. The flakes were fat and floaty. The ground was quickly getting moist, muddy and slippery. We had to return to the cabin and there could be no delay because we new the area when wet turned into a bottomless mud bog, sure to suck your tires up to the door jams. We were at least ten miles out with no desire to walk in. Still, it was a fun, bouncy, fast, slippery ride. We laughed and joked all the way as we would on a holiday slay-ride through a snowy forest full of ugly nymphs.

When we got to the cabin, CM's Grandma came running out all excited.

"Grandpa has not returned. I don't know what to think. He's all alone. He said he would be back no later than noon and it is two o'clock now! You have to go find him!"

The snow was coming down heavier and accumulating fast. It was already six inches deep and it had only been snowing for a little over an hour. The clouds were dark, heavy and moving very slowly overhead. We thought that CM should stay and eat and warm up while we went to look for his gramps but he would not.

"I'm the one that has the permit. You said I could shoot first. I can catch one in the snow! We can track him until I get him," He exclaimed.

"And, besides I need to help find Gramps."

We could not deny his kind of enthusiasm and excitement and sense of responsibility.

"That is why they call it hunting. It is a lot of work. You have to learn to live in it, survive it, and like the elements," CM's dad surmised.

"Yeah, come on! He's right! We hunt until it is dark, until we can't see 'em in our sights." I said.

So, off we went, eastward into the flats where the ground is less rocky and more boggy, watery and sticky.

"We'll be burning some gasoline to keep the tires moving out there. Buckle up so your head doesn't bang into the cab roof, and hang on!" our driver instructed.

"By the way, did you grab the shovel next to the fire pit?"

"Nope." CM and I said at the same time.

Then we laughed but were truly hoping we would not get stuck and need a shovel as we drove up and down and all around, stopping every ten or twenty minutes to yell gramps' name. The yelling was not the best thing to do while hunting but we had our priorities. Still, the sun was going down, the air freezing and we had no luck at locating our late hunter.

We decided that we had to go back to the cabin, check in, and get some dry warmer cloths, lanterns, flashlights, food, the shovel, and a topographic map of the specific area. When we arrived, there was Gramps, safe and sound and warm inside the place drinking some tea. Boy, were we relieved.

Gramps had taken a bearing of the land and the landmarks in each direction the day before, just as I had. He knew the ridge behind the cabin ran the full length of plateau and when it began to snow, the trail he was walking was lost so he cut across country and walked back just under the ridge, to the cabin. It was the longer way back but the safer way—and smarter choice.

The next morning at sunrise, the ground was covered with snow. Tracks were everywhere and the elk had ventured very near our cabin. Dad, first one to rise, got dressed and went outside. He ran back into the cabin before he could slam the door shut from his exit.

"Get up! Get up fast and get dressed! There is a herd of elk on the ridge behind the cabin!"

We scampered, fell into the sides of the walls, tripped around and over sleeping bodies that had not moved yet. Cloths were being slung all over the room, while trying to find the right ones. It hurt to bend and tie the boots because the blood was rushing and the excitement so high that I could not breathe. My socks were not on right, the heel on the upside. I did not take the time to turn them, something I thought about because they might hurt later. I hoped that my shirt was right side out as I slung on my down coat.

Dad, CM and I ran up the ridge, the elk in sight all the while. Before us a herd of elk were meandering through the trees, scraping the snow with hoofs, eating the wet grass, moving slowly along as they ate. The wetness of the morning silenced our movement. It was foggy and that helped hide us from the grazing elk herd. The air so still and heavy that it felt like a wonderland only described in fairytales when magical things happen.

It was magical alright, witnessed when the fog rose and elk just appeared as if from nowhere, only twenty yards in front of us.

"CM, get over here. Sit down in between my legs. Lean next to my chest. Use my arms and knees as a rest!" Dad whispered while pulling CM into position, both dropping to the ground at the same time.

In front of CM was a big cow and following her, a yearling calf. We could see puffs of steam coming out of their nostrils that made long pencil like streaks that floated up and into the air. The cow licked a leaf and it sort of stuck to her tong making her rub her tong against her teeth and upper lip. I could see the dew drops on the Outer ends of the hair on her mane.

"Quit breathing!" CM said out loud in frustration.

"You're making my gun go up and down. I can't shoot because you are making my rifle swoop and wave!"

I watched as dad held his breath and the rifle barrel drop down to the evenly lined up position while CM took aim. Then dad breathed again, and CM turned to give him the evil eye.

Then they started discussing which one to shoot. CM decided as he moved his aim from the big cow and took new aim on the calf.

That surprised me.

It seemed to me, that there was too much talking going on and that all of the getting ready, deciding, and doing was taking way too long. If there was going to be a shot taken, it better happen within the next second or two.

"Ka-Boom!"

"He's down!" I yelled as if they could not see it was, as the little tiny jack pine they were leaning against shook from the recoil, spattering dad and CM with dusts of snow.

The herd ran in all directions reacting to the sudden loud noise made by the shot and my loud voice. Dad and CM did not even twitch for a few seconds then they both swatted at their ears and the back of their necks realizing the freezing tickles from the snow dusting they got.

"It's time for the killin' jig!" I screamed as they scampered to their feet.

"What's that?" CM asked.

"Well, first you go the animal. You poke it with your gun barrel. Look at it. Touch it. Open its mouth and pull out its tongue to look at it. Rub its head. Sit on its back. Get up. Look at it some more. Then it hits you. You shake hands if there is anybody with you and jump up and down and turn in circles and yell and laugh until the adrenalin stops running through your body," I explained.

We all did that and then dropped to the ground on our rears, and grinned at each other for a long time.

"I saw you turn your aim from the cow to the calf, why'd you do that?" I asked.

CM looked thoughtful, staring at the sky and hem-hawin' and shifting his weight around. I thought he was thinking we would be mad at him. Then he explained.

"The cow was too big. The calf was more my size. I didn't want to shoot the momma. And, I could see more of the little one in my scope. And dad was breathing so hard and shaking my gun and by the time he stopped, the calf was right in front of me."

Dad and I just hugged him, shook his hand and squeezed his shoulder while we declared what a great decision he made and what a great shot he took. What a great time—a memory of a lifetime made—priceless—extraordinary event. History made! The beginning of a life-time passion had come upon us. We were feeling proud of him and grateful to be a part of it all. We laughed and hugged again.

Then the work started.

Dressing a calf out is as hard as any bigger animal. In fact, a calf elk is larger than a big deer so it is the same work no matter what size the animal. CM did it himself with only a little assistance from his dad and I and our assistance was more directive than hands-on. He did not like it all but he figured he needed to learn if he was going to hunt and he thought it was the man-thing to do.

"You guys are doing so well by yourselves. It's a down hill drag on snow to the cabin. The snow is lightly falling again—perfect for tracking and hunting. I'm going on, to the top of the ridge and work it back to where the mountain makes a saddle cut, then I'll come down the cut. I'll meet you back at the cabin later." I explained while grabbing my gun, backpack and other gear. So, off I went by myself.

By the time I reached the ridge just off the top, it was so beautiful all around me that I had to stop and gaze up at the giant snowflakes falling from heaven. Everything around me is pristine, clean, quiet, serene—so serene that I know I am privileged to be in that spot at that moment in time. It was breezy and the temperature had to be in the teens which made me realize every inch of my skin but it just does not get any better.

As I walked along I heard elk busting out just under my location. Oak bush limbs snapped. Hooves made knocking sounds as they trampled through the snow on top of rocks. That was exciting. Every ten yards I crunched down, wiped my scope and peered through the snowy forest below me, my 7 magnum rifle ready to shoot, waiting and hoping to catch a bull walking around. To know that I am in the middle of these big animals, walking in the same direction, sneaking around just out of sight and breath is exhilarating. There is no time, no clock ticking. No other person, nothing except the animals and me and God. I was having delusions of adequacy.

I was reaching the saddle area and decided to drop down the ridge and angle down to the cut area where the two mountain ridges meet. I had only gone a few steps when I spied a big animal lying next to a cedar tree's trunk, the head looking downward, staring and not a twitch in the body to be seen. I knew it was an elk but could not tell if it was cow or bull from where I stood in shock.

I could not think of what I should do next.

I wonder why it shocks me, seeing what I am hunting for. It just does. It is the same way I feel when a fish bites my hook, I feel shocked and surprised because the hook is so small and the fish are too scarce and there is too much other food in the water for a fish to bite a little worm hooked on the end of an invisible line.

Finally, it hit me. Lock and load, aim and be ready to shoot. Something inside of my head said, "You can use the scope to see if it is a bull. Never your binoculars if you can shoot."

Enlightened, I did just that and could tell immediately that it was a bull elk. It had a small rack that had been broken off just above the first fork or it is a spike or his mass could be hiding in the low cedar limbs. I decided that small did not bother me. It would be my first bull elk, absolutely excellent for eating all winter.

Looking through my scope I could only see the ends of his hair sticking up. It was like looking through a kaleidoscope: the hairs on his back sparkling, prism-like light glistening and twinkling while it blew in the wind. Iridescent colors danced around inside the circle space in my scope that I was peering through. The snow was flying and the flakes were big and wet and I could see them hit the hairs and dissipate at the same time. Every other second a snowflake landed on the outside of the end of my scope and dripped very slowly down, puddling on the metal rim.

I could not think of what to do but I did realize that I needed to change my focus and concentrate and that I should not be thinking about the little magical things happening because those thoughts were putting me under a spell of wonderment and stupidity.

I moved the scope view to the head area and found the tip of the bull's ear. I slowly dropped the rifle using the scope cross-hairs as a guide to move my aim straight down and when I got to the base of the ear, I dropped my sight a little lower and decided to pull the trigger.

"Ka-Boom!" the shot sounded.

I froze for a second then I remembered to eject the shell and reload to be ready to shoot again if the bull jumped to his hooves. The snow was falling so heavily that I could not see the bull but I thought I would have if he had moved. It was like a cloud had dropped between the bull and me. I had to think, how cool was that?

Poof! A little breeze floated by and I could see the elk lying there, like a frozen statue. I was not sure I hit him with my bullet. After all I did not see him fall and I actually only saw his ear and only the tip of that for sure. He looked like he was knapping, just as before. I decided to sneak up closer.

While sneaking, tip-toeing in the snow, I found and picked up a long stick, about sixteen feet long and stuck it under my arm like a lance, draping it over the top of my elbow while I had my hand on the fore barrel and my other hand's finger on the trigger. I probably looked really stupid.

Closer, closer, close enough then I poked him with the stick. He did not move. That is when I deduced that I got him and walked closer to check. Sure enough, he was dead. My bullet hit just one inch below the base of his right ear; deadliest shot that could be made.

Wow! Excitement and realization of what I accomplished thrilled me. I just started yelling, "I got him! I got him!"

"Help!"

Help? I wondered why I said that and a joy kind of laughter over took me.

"I am all alone up on this ridge. Now what am I suppose to do?"

I used my binoculars and could see people walking about and around the cabin far below. I could also see that a couple of them were using their binoculars, scanning exactly where I stood in a little opening. I could see that CM and his dad had made it back and they were working on the calf, skinning it out in the snow. Little sister was running around gathering and making snowballs that she was throwing at CM but he was ignoring her. Grandma was playfully looking around at all the activity around her. She looked like she was having a wonderful time. I knew that they had to have heard the shot and they would most likely know it was me that shot.

I got my long stick and tied a red scarf at the tip and waved it around above the little treetops but I could tell that they could not see it.

The next thing to do was to get my bull gutted so that he would cool then I would have to go get help.

I tied his legs to trees on each side of the elk and discovered that he was too big to roll over. No matter what I did, I could not move him to where I could efficiently do the dastardly deed completely. I propped the stick with the scarf tied to it against a tree, sort of stuck into the frozen ground where there was a slight opening on the downhill side thinking that would help mark the area and so that I could find the place again when I returned.

I started my descent and as I did, I tied florescent orange plastic survey tape strips to branches to mark my trail. It was still snowing and I knew it would be difficult to locate exactly where my elk lay. My track could easily be covered with snow by the time I returned.

I had walked half way down the mountain when I heard someone call my name and turned to walk toward whoever it was. Shorty, I met up with CM's gramps. We greeted, I excitedly told him what had happened and that my bull was up there just waiting to be retrieved. We both made our way back to the elk.

It was such a struggle to manage moving the elk into a better cleaning position and we were arguing about what and how it should be done.

"One of us has to leave and get off this mountain! It can be you or me but I've had just about enough of you telling me what to do!" Gramps finally declared.

"Come on! That can't be right!" I said.

I could not believe that he was painstakingly tying little strings of red yarn into perfect little bows about an inch apart onto the exposed urine and colon tubes.

"What in the world are you thinking?"

I had never seen that done before and just could not believe he was doing it! I was also miffed at the cute little bows he made.

"Why not tie knots? That's the biggest waste of time I have ever seen!"

I guessed the bows were made because he planned to pull and undo the bows at some point in the cleaning process. It just amazed me and for some reason, I found it very annoying. I wanted to get bloody and rip and get and be done with the exhausting chore right away.

"I'll go!"

I grabbed my coat and gloves that I had removed for the cleaning process. Strapped my gear around my waist and slung my rifle over my shoulder. Then

I disappeared into the forest thinking that he could tie all the little stupid red bows he wanted to! I will do the double hike.

As I walked, I decided that everything that had happened since I left CM and his dad had been stupid-stupid-stupid and the red-bow thing was just the icing on the whole stupid thing. Still, I had gotten my elk and he was a beauty and I was so proud of myself and I was thinking about what parts of the story to tell and not tell, to the others. That is when it dawned on me that I should have turned my scope power down. I might have been able to actually see the body of the elk if I had thought to do that. Stupid-stupid and I decided that I was not going to tell that part of the story right away. The important thing is that I figured it out and I did it very well and creatively and I had shot my very first elk, a bull elk!

I arrived at the cabin in a short time. CM, his dad and Joe who had just arrived at camp, joined me. All the hands and backs to help carry the elk were welcome.

CM's dad is a veteran hunter, one who has expertise and wisdom when it comes to cleaning and retrieving wild animals. I chuckled as I pointed out the elk laying on the ground and Gramps who was standing over it looking proud. CM's dad began laughing like I had never heard him do before as he approached the elk.

Catching his breathe in between his laughing, CM's dad asked, "What in the world is this?" while pointing to the twenty or so, little tiny perfectly tied red yarn bows inside of the cavity. The tied tubes were rolled up ever so neatly like a garden hose.

"It's so I could keep them from leaking while I cut them out from this end," Gramps explained pointing to the rear end.

"Well, I've never seen that technique before. I do it this way!" CM's dad replied as he knelt down to skillfully show us how to do it.

In less than five minutes that job was done. Then he climbed inside of the animal, cut the diaphragm loose blindly with his knife, which released all other matter finishing the cleaning job. Then we skinned the elk and quartered the animal. We loaded our packs, shoulders and arms with meat, hide, rack, and our gear and descended off the mountain.

Everybody was in a happy, snow-play disposition. We could not help but run and slide down on our rears at every opportunity. Besides, it was slippery and we fell down often so sliding was easier than fighting it. We were all laughing when we reached the bottom and we took a little time to wipe off the snow stuck to our cloths and shake the wet out of our hair and to adjust the weight distribution of our packs while we looked at each other widely smiling.

Dinner was so delicious that evening. Grandma had managed to cook a pot roast with biscuits, gravy, green beans, carrots, and potatoes and an apple cobbler for dessert which all came out of that amazing wood burning cook stove.

The warmness of the dinner and the family and events of the day could never feel or be better.

The next day, CM, his dad and I joined the other two hunters who still needed to bag their elk. Joe had his son with him and shot a big cow on top of the same ridge that I shot mine on. Being his first elk made it extra special. The cleaning and packing was difficult because the day before we had done the same with mine but sore bodies were not the main reason for our stress.

It was bitterly cold that day when we gathered at the top of the mountain to help pack it out. It was so cold that a match would not strike. We struggled over forty-five minutes trying to get a little fire lit so we could warm our bare cold hands. The wood was too cold to light and burn. It was so cold that whiskers froze on faces. Our face cheeks could not move because they were frozen, making words was hard so we did not talk. It was so cold that icicles formed on the rims of the knitted beanie caps pulled over ears. It was so cold that I wondered if I would survive through the day. The snow storm had cleared out, the wind was blowing in twenty mile an hour gusts, and the cold-cold had settled on the land and upon us.

Once we had that elk stowed, we had all had enough adventure for that day and did not venture out again. Instead we stayed warm inside the cabin, played cards, told stories and we ate and drank the rest of the day, and slept soundly through the night.

The next morning was Thanksgiving Day and we were very thankful that the wind had stopped blowing and it was sunny. It felt like a heat-wave had come through, raising the temperature to thirty degrees outside.

Gramps held the only tag left that had not been filled; CM and his dad left with Gramps at sunrise to hunt. Grandma started the holiday dinner and whiffs of delicious smells twirled though the air once the stove smoke broke the roofline and floated into the prairie area where we were working, scraping the inside of the elk hides with obsidian chips and our hunting knives.

We were using obsidian, the hard black shiny rock that Indians fashioned arrowheads of. We found the scraper shaped wedges with sharp edges on the ridge. For the scraping job the best piece is as big as the palm of a grown-up hand. One holds the rock at an angle scraping the inside of the hide in the manner you would pet a dog. That is the way the Indians did it and we were into doing things that day, as they did them in the olden days. It did not work very well. Knives are much better tools to use but we thought we'd give it a try. It was nice to have snow on the ground to spread the hides out upon to do this chore.

Because it was Thanksgiving Day, we thought and talked about American history, killing wild animals for food, braving the weather, working happily and contentedly together. I know we were actually catching wild, life-living our heritage and a ten-year-old crossed over a new threshold, completing his right of passage.